HSPT
PREP BOOK
FOR CATHOLIC HIGH SCHOOLS

The Comprehensive Study Guide for Middle School Students to Ace the Entrance Exam with Practice Tests, Detailed Answer Explanations, and Proven Strategies

© Copyright 2025 - Hanley Publications LLC All rights reserved.

It is not legal to reproduce, duplicate, or transmit any part of this document in either electronic means or in printed format. Recording of this publication is strictly prohibited and any storage of this document is not allowed unless with written permission from the publisher except for the use of brief quotations in a book review.

This book is a work of fiction. Any resemblance to persons, living or dead, or places, events or locations is purely coincidental.

All rights reserved. This book or any portion thereof may not be reproduced or used in any manner whatsoever without the express written permission of the publisher except for the use of brief quotations in a book review.

First edition, 2024.

Contents

Introduction 1

Chapter One: About the HSPT 2
    The Purpose of the HSPT 2
    Content of the HSPT 3
    Where to Take the HSPT Exam 15
    HSPT Scoring: Understanding Your Results 16
    How to Prepare for the HSPT 17

Chapter Two: Reading Comprehension 19
    Types of Reading Comprehension Questions 19
    Practice Passage 1: Using the Four Question Types 21
    Detail and Main Idea Questions 24
    Practice Passage 2: Detail and Main Idea Questions 26
    Inference and Vocabulary Questions 28
    Practice Passage 3: Inference and Vocabulary Questions 30

Chapter Three: Vocabulary 33
    Kinds of Vocabulary Questions 33
    Synonym Questions 34
    Antonym Questions 36
    Context Questions 38
    Word Parts 41
    Confusing Words 46
    More Vocabulary Practice 47

Chapter Four: Language Skills 54
What HSPT Usage Questions Are Like 54
Sentences 55
Mastering Verbs 58
Clear Sentences 59
HSPT Punctuation and Capitalization 61
HSPT Spelling 67
HSPT Composition 70

Chapter Five: Verbal and Nonverbal Reasoning 75
Verbal Analogies 75
HSPT Number Series 82
Geometric and Non Geometric Comparison 85

Chapter Six: Math Skills 93
Word Problems 93
Number Names 99
Fraction Problems 102
Decimals 120
Percents 129
Averages 135
Length, Weight, and Time Units: 137
Algebra 141
Positive and Negative Numbers 143
Squares and Square Roots 147
Perimeter, Area, and the Pythagorean Theorem 158
The Pythagorean Theorem 166

Chapter Seven: HSPT Exam 1 169
Part 1: Verbal Skills 169
Part 2: Quantitative Skills 181
Part 3: Reading Skills 195
Part 4: Mathematics 213
Part 5: Language Skills 228
Answer Key Verbal Skills 243
Answer Key Quantitative Skills 245
Answer Key Reading Skills 247

Answer Key Mathematics 249
Answer Key Language Skills 251

Chapter Eight: Answers and Explanation of HSPT Exam 1 252
Part 1: Verbal Skills 252
Part 2: Quantitative Skills 261
Part 3: Reading Skills 268
Part 4: Mathematics 274
Part 5: Language Skills 283

Conclusion 291

References 292

Free Video Offer!

Thank you for purchasing from Hanley Test Preparation! We're honored to help you prepare for your exam. To show our appreciation, we're offering an Exclusive Test Tips Video.

This video includes multiple strategies that will make you successful on your big exam.

All we ask is that you email us your feedback and describe your experience with our product. Amazing, awful, or just so-so. We want to hear what you have to say!

To get your FREE VIDEO, just send us an email at bonusvideo@hanleytestprep.com with **Free Video** in the subject line and the following information in the body of the email:

- The name of the product you purchased
- Your product rating on a scale of 1-5, with 5 being the highest rating.
- Your feedback about the product.

If you have any questions or concerns, please don't hesitate to contact us at support@hanleytestprep.com

Thanks again!

Introduction

Welcome to the HSPT Prep Book 2025-2026 for Catholic Schools! This comprehensive study guide is designed to help you excel in your preparation for the High School Placement Test (HSPT). Inside, you'll find over 700 practice questions, detailed answer explanations, and a full-length model exam to give you a realistic preview of what to expect on test day. Whether you're aiming for top-tier Catholic schools or want to boost your confidence, this study guide offers the strategies and resources you need to succeed. Without further delay; let's dive in and help you prepare today.

Chapter One: About the HSPT

The High School Placement Test (HSPT) stands as a significant benchmark in your academic journey, designed to assess your readiness for the challenges of high school. Taken by thousands of eighth-grade students across the United States, the HSPT evaluates a diverse set of skills to provide schools with a comprehensive understanding of their academic strengths. Whether you are stepping into a Catholic high school or another private institution, the HSPT is your opportunity to showcase your abilities and secure a solid foundation for your educational future.

The Purpose of the HSPT

The HSPTs primary purpose is to evaluate your preparedness for the academic rigor of high school. By testing a range of critical skills across five core areas, the exam ensures that schools can accurately determine how well you are equipped to succeed in subjects such as mathematics, reading, and verbal reasoning. The results not only help schools place you in the appropriate courses but may also be used to identify eligibility for advanced programs or scholarships.

The HSPT's structure is designed to challenge your ability to think critically, solve problems effectively, and apply foundational knowledge to complex scenarios. This makes the test a measure of your current skills and a predictor of your potential for future academic success.

Content of the HSPT

The HSPT is a timed exam that spans two and a half hours and includes 298 questions divided across five skill areas. Each section of the test plays a unique role in painting a holistic picture of your capabilities. Let's take a closer look at the structure and purpose of its components:

1. **Verbal Skills**: This section measures your ability to understand and analyze language. It includes tasks like verbal analogies, synonyms, and logic-based questions. These are designed to test your reasoning skills, vocabulary, and ability to identify relationships between ideas.

2. **Quantitative Skills**: This segment evaluates your mathematical reasoning and problem-solving abilities. It challenges you to recognize patterns, work with numbers, and think critically about mathematical concepts.

3. **Reading**: The reading section assesses your comprehension skills, focusing on how well you can extract meaning from written passages and interpret information accurately.

4. **Mathematics**: This part tests your understanding of fundamental math concepts, ranging from basic arithmetic to introductory algebra and geometry. It ensures you're ready for the level of math taught in high school.

5. **Language**: The language section focuses on grammar, punctuation, and sentence structure, evaluating how effectively you can use and understand the mechanics of written English.

Sub-tests	Number of Questions	Time Allotted
Verbal Skills	60	16 minutes
Quantitative Skills	52	30 minutes
Reading	62	25 minutes
Mathematics	64	45 minutes
Language Skills	60	25 minutes

Optional Tests

While the HSPT itself includes these five core areas, some schools may require optional sections on science, mechanical aptitude, or Catholic religion. These additional components are school-specific and not universally mandated. Since they fall outside the scope of the standard HSPT, they are not covered in this guide.

Unlike other standardized tests, the HSPT doesn't simply focus on memorization. Instead, it challenges you to apply your knowledge creatively and analytically. Each question is designed to test how well you can use the skills you've learned in real-world scenarios, making it a well-rounded measure of your academic preparedness.

Part 1: Verbal Skills

The Verbal Skills section of the HSPT is your chance to showcase your ability to think critically, reason effectively, and work with language at a high level. It's a dynamic part of the test designed to measure more than just vocabulary—it evaluates how well you understand relationships between ideas, classify concepts, and draw logical conclusions. With a total of 60 questions, this section challenges different aspects of your verbal reasoning abilities. Let's dive into the key components of this section and uncover how each part plays a crucial role in assessing your skills.

1. Verbal Analogies (10 Questions)

Verbal analogies go beyond simple word definitions. These questions challenge your ability to recognize relationships between words and ideas and apply that understanding to new contexts. You will encounter a pair of related words, followed by a third word and four answer choices. Your task is to select the word that completes the second set to match the relationship of the first pair.

For example:

Hand is to glove as foot is to...?

(a) sock (b) shoe (c) sandal (d) boot

The ability to solve verbal analogies demonstrates your capacity for critical thinking and abstract reasoning. As you practice, remember to focus on identifying the exact nature of the relationship in the first pair before applying it to the second. Chapter 5, Verbal and Non Verbal Reasoning, provides a detailed breakdown of analogy strategies and practice examples to help you master this skill.

2. Synonyms (15 Questions)

Synonym questions test the depth and breadth of your vocabulary by asking you to identify a word that most closely matches the meaning of a given word. These questions not only reflect your familiarity with language but also assess your ability to discern subtle differences between words with similar meanings.

For example:

Select the synonym for the word 'brilliant':

(a) smart (b) dazzling (c) intelligent (d) vivid

The key to excelling in this section is understanding context and word nuances. Strong vocabulary skills are invaluable, and Chapter 3, Vocabulary, offers tips and techniques to enhance your word knowledge effectively.

3. Antonyms (9 Questions)

In contrast to synonyms, antonym questions require you to identify the word that has the opposite meaning to the given word. These questions challenge your ability to think in reverse, an important skill in language comprehension and reasoning.

For example:

Select the antonym for the word 'generous':

(a) selfish (b) wealthy (c) kind (d) extravagant

Antonym questions push you to not only know a word's meaning but also its contextually opposite idea. Chapter 3, Vocabulary, also covers strategies for tackling antonym questions, ensuring you are well-prepared for this segment.

4. Logic (10 Questions)

Logic questions are where verbal reasoning meets critical thinking. These questions test your ability to evaluate whether a third statement is true, false, or uncertain based on two provided statements.

For example:
Statement 1: All cats are mammals.
Statement 2: Some mammals are dogs.

Is the following statement true, false, or uncertain? All dogs are cats.

Logic questions require sharp focus and an ability to break down relationships systematically. They emphasize structured reasoning over intuition, helping to determine your analytical abilities. You'll find detailed explanations and examples in Chapter 5, Verbal and Non Verbal Reasoning.

5. Verbal Classification (16 Questions)

Verbal classification questions challenge both your vocabulary and reasoning skills. Each question presents a group of four words, and you must determine which one doesn't belong based on shared traits or categories.

For example:

Which word does not belong?

(a) apple (b) orange (c) banana (d) lettuce

To excel in this section, focus on identifying patterns or categories shared by the majority of the words and finding the outlier. These questions are as much about reasoning as they are about vocabulary, and Chapter 5, Verbal and Non Verbal Reasoning, covers them in detail.

Part-2 Quantitative Skills Breakdown

The Quantitative Skills section of the HSPT is where you test your numerical reasoning and nonverbal thinking abilities. This part of the test challenges your ability to identify patterns, compare quantities, and manipulate numbers—all essential skills for problem-solving in both academic and real-world contexts. With a total of 52 questions, this section is carefully crafted to assess how well you think critically and analytically when working with numbers and shapes. Let's explore the four distinct components of the Quantitative Skills section and how each evaluates your aptitude.

1. Number Series (18 Questions)

Number series questions test your ability to recognize patterns and predict what comes next. In each question, you'll be given a sequence of numbers arranged in a specific logical order. Your task is to determine the next number in the sequence from four given options.

For example:

What comes next in the series:

2, 4, 8, 16?

(a) 20 (b) 24 (c) 32 (d) 40

To excel in this section, focus on identifying the rule governing the series. Is it addition, multiplication, or something more complex? Success in number series questions demonstrates your capacity to spot trends and think sequentially, both crucial skills for tackling higher-level math. Chapter 5, Verbal and Nonverbal Reasoning, provides detailed examples and strategies to master these questions.

2. Geometric Comparison (9 Questions)

In geometric comparison questions, numbers take a backseat as shapes and visual reasoning take the spotlight. You'll be presented with three geometric figures and asked quantitative questions about their properties. These questions might involve identifying which figure has more of a particular characteristic, which has less, or which is equal to a given attribute.

For example:

Which figure has the largest area?

(a) Triangle (b) Square (c) Circle (d) Rectangle

This component tests your ability to evaluate and compare shapes based on visual and spatial reasoning. It's about understanding proportions, sizes, and relationships between geometric figures. Chapter 5, Verbal and *Nonverbal Reasoning*, dives deeper into the tricks and techniques for solving these questions.

3. Nongeometric Comparison (8 Questions)

Nongeometric comparison questions take you back to numerical reasoning. You'll be presented with three numerical statements and asked questions that require you to compare these numbers.

For example:

Which number is the largest?

(a) 5 x 4 (b) 9 + 3 (c) 12 ÷ 2 (d) 20 − 6

Here, quick mental math and attention to detail are key. These questions test your ability to calculate accurately and compare results efficiently. By practicing these, you'll develop your skills in breaking down quantitative relationships at a glance.

4. Number Manipulation (17 Questions)

Number manipulation is the heart of mathematical problem-solving. In this component, you'll perform mathematical operations—such as addition, subtraction, multiplication, and division—to arrive at the correct answer from four choices.

For example:

What is the result of 15 + (3 x 4)?

(a) 27 (b) 51(c) 72 (d) 60

These questions assess your ability to apply basic math concepts while following the rules of arithmetic operations, including the order of operations. Mastery of this section showcases your confidence in working with numbers under time constraints. For detailed tips and example problems, see Chapter 6, *Math Skills*.

Part 3: Reading Skills Breakdown

The Reading Skills section of the HSPT measures how effectively you can understand, analyze, and interpret written language. This part of the exam doesn't just assess your ability to recall information but also evaluates your critical thinking and comprehension skills—abilities that are essential for success in high school and beyond. With 62 total questions divided into **Comprehension** and **Vocabulary**, this section offers a dynamic mix of tasks to showcase your reading prowess. Let's dive into what each component compromises and how it helps you excel as a reader.

1. Comprehension (40 Questions)

The comprehension component is the centerpiece of the Reading Skills section. Here, you will encounter passages of varying lengths and subjects, ranging from factual to literary. After reading each passage, you'll answer questions that challenge different facets of your understanding.

You might be asked to:

- **Identify key facts**: Spot specific details directly mentioned in the text.
- **Draw conclusions**: Make logical inferences based on the information provided.
- **Analyze authorial intent**: Determine why the author wrote the passage and what they aimed to convey.

For example:

Passage Excerpt: "The rainforest is home to an astonishing variety of plant and animal species, many of which remain undiscovered."

Question: What is the main idea of the passage?

(a) Rainforests are disappearing.
(b) Many species in the rainforest are still unknown.
(c) Animals live in rainforests.
(d) Rainforests are smaller than deserts.

Your ability to interact with a passage—to understand both the explicit and implicit ideas—forms the backbone of your reading comprehension skills. Chapter 2, *Reading Comprehension*, offers in-depth strategies to navigate this section, including skimming for key points and identifying context clues.

2. Vocabulary (22 Questions)

Vocabulary questions assess the breadth and depth of your word knowledge. In this component, you'll encounter sentences with an underlined word, and your job is to select from four choices the word that most closely matches the meaning of the underlined term.

For example:

Sentence: The teacher's explanation was both *concise* and clear.

Question: What does the word *concise* most nearly mean?

(a) Lengthy (b) Brief (c) Confusing (d) Friendly

This section goes beyond simple memorization. It evaluates your ability to understand words in context and to recognize synonyms. Success here reflects your linguistic awareness, an asset not just for the test but for high school reading and writing. To strengthen your vocabulary and refine your skills for this portion of the exam, turn to Chapter 3, Vocabulary, which provides targeted practice and effective learning techniques.

Part 4: Mathematics Breakdown

The Mathematics Skills section of the HSPT is designed to assess your mastery of core mathematical concepts and your ability to apply them effectively in problem-solving scenarios. This section not only evaluates your numerical proficiency but also gauges how well you understand the logic and principles behind mathematical problems. With 64 questions divided between Concepts and Problem Solving, this section invites you to showcase both your theoretical understanding and practical application of math. Let's explore each component in detail.

1. Concepts (24 Questions)

The Concepts component focuses on the fundamental principles that underpin mathematical reasoning. These questions challenge you to identify the rules or concepts that explain a given problem. Instead of simply solving for an answer, you'll demonstrate your understanding of why certain mathematical processes work.

For example:

Question: Why does dividing a number by a fraction result in a larger number?

(a) Because the numerator becomes smaller
(b) Because you are multiplying by the reciprocal
(c) Because fractions are always smaller than whole numbers
(d) Because the denominator is larger than the numerator

This part of the exam requires you to think beyond calculations and consider the "why" behind the math. By mastering this component, you'll not only excel on the HSPT but also strengthen your foundational math skills, which will serve you in advanced courses like algebra, geometry, and beyond. Chapter 6, Math Skills, provides a detailed review of the key concepts you'll need, along with examples to help solidify your understanding.

2. Problem Solving (40 Questions)

The Problem Solving component tests your ability to apply mathematical knowledge to real-world problems. You'll encounter a variety of scenarios, ranging from straightforward arithmetic to more complex word problems, each designed to evaluate your ability to analyze, calculate, and determine the correct solution.

For example:

Question: A car travels 60 miles in 1.5 hours. What is its average speed in miles per hour?

(a) 40 (b) 45 (c) 50 (d) 60

These questions require sharp focus, quick calculations, and a knack for breaking down problems into manageable steps. Whether you're calculating percentages, working with ratios, or solving equations, this section emphasizes practical math skills that are directly relevant to high school coursework. Chapter 6, Math Skills, offers a wealth of practice problems and strategies to ensure you're prepared to tackle these challenges confidently.

Part 5: Language Skills Breakdown

The Language Skills section of the HSPT serves as the ultimate test of your command of English mechanics, grammar, spelling, and composition. This section evaluates how well you understand and apply the rules that govern clear, effective written communication. With 60 questions divided across four key areas—Punctuation and Capitalization, Usage, Spelling, and Composition—this section gives you the chance to demonstrate your attention to detail and ability to craft polished, precise language. Let's dive into each component to uncover what you can expect and how to excel.

1. Punctuation and Capitalization (12 Questions)

This component ensures you know the rules of punctuation and capitalization that keep sentences crisp and clear. You'll analyze three sentences to identify errors, ranging from missing commas to improper capitalization of proper nouns. If no errors are present, your answer will be the fourth option: "No mistakes."

Example question types may include:

- Identifying a missing apostrophe in a contraction.
- Spotting a misplaced capital letter in a common noun.
- Detecting an incorrectly used homophone (e.g., their vs. there).

Mastering this skill is essential for crafting error-free sentences. Chapter 8, Language Skills, provides all the examples and explanations you need to approach these questions with confidence.

2. Usage (28 Questions)

Grammar is the backbone of effective communication, and the Usage component tests how well you understand it. From subject-verb agreement to pronoun consistency, these questions cover the essential elements of English syntax. Similar to the punctuation questions, you'll analyze three sentences to locate errors in grammar or usage—or choose "No mistakes" if the sentences are correct.

This component emphasizes your ability to apply rules in real-world contexts. Questions might involve:

- Choosing the correct verb form to match a subject.
- Identifying incorrect pronoun usage in a sentence.
- Identifying the misuse of an adjective where an adverb is needed.

By refining your grammar knowledge with the guidance in Chapter 8, you'll be equipped to tackle these questions like a seasoned writer.

3. Spelling (10 Questions)

The HSPT measures your ability to recognize misspelled words is key. For these questions, you'll evaluate three sentences to pinpoint a spelling error or confirm that all words are correct with the fourth option, "No mistakes."

Expect to encounter questions that test your familiarity with commonly misspelled words, homophones, and irregular spellings. For example:

- Distinguishing between "their," "there," and "they're."
- Spotting a misspelling in a complex word like "accommodation."
- Identifying the incorrect use of "its" versus "it's."

Spelling is a skill that never goes out of style, and Chapter 8 will help you polish yours with helpful tips and practice.

4. Composition (10 Questions)

The Composition component challenges you to think critically about how sentences and paragraphs are structured. You'll be asked to choose:

- The best word or phrase to connect two ideas.
- The sentence that most effectively conveys a thought.
- The sentence that doesn't belong in a paragraph.

This section is all about recognizing effective writing. For example, you might need to select the best transitional phrase to link two related ideas or identify a sentence that disrupts the flow of a paragraph.

Through these questions, you'll demonstrate your ability to evaluate and improve the quality of written communication—a vital skill for both academic and personal success. Chapter 8 is your go-to resource for mastering the art of composition.

Where to Take the HSPT Exam

One of the first steps on your journey to high school success is determining where you'll take the High School Placement Test (HSPT). The process is straightforward, but it's also a crucial step that ensures you're fully prepared when exam day arrives. Here's how to get started:

The HSPT is administered at the schools you're considering attending. To find out where and when your exam will take place, simply call the admissions office of one of the schools on your list. Schools offering the HSPT are experienced in guiding students and parents through the process, so don't hesitate to ask any questions you may have.

- **What to ask:**
    - Confirm the date and time of the exam.
    - Ask about any specific requirements, such as bringing ID or other materials.
    - Inquire if they provide any additional resources or guidelines to help you prepare.

Knowing the exact location and timing of your exam well in advance is vital for reducing pre-test stress and ensuring you arrive fully prepared. Some schools might also offer tours or open house events on the same day, giving you a chance to explore the environment you could soon call your academic home.

> *Pro Tip: If you're applying to multiple schools, make sure you're clear about which school's HSPT results will be shared with the others. This eliminates any confusion later on.*

HSPT Scoring: Understanding Your Results

The High School Placement Test (HSPT) scoring system is designed not just to evaluate your performance but to give schools a well-rounded view of your academic abilities. Understanding how the scoring works is key to approaching the test with confidence and a clear strategy. Let's break it down step by step.

Your HSPT score is determined solely by the number of questions you answer correctly. The good news? **Wrong answers don't count against you.** This means there's no penalty for guessing, so it's always worth taking a shot at every question.

Once the Scholastic Testing Service (STS)—the creators of the HSPT—collects your answers, they calculate your raw score (the total number of correct responses). This raw score is then converted into a **standard score** on a scale of 200 to 800.

Your HSPT score report contains several important pieces of information:

1. **Standard Scores**: Your performance on each section of the test, compared against the standard 200–800 scale.
2. **Percentile Ranks**: Both **national** and **local percentiles** show how your scores compare to students across the country and within your area. For example, a national percentile rank of 85 means you performed better than 85% of test-takers nationwide.
3. **Grade Equivalent**: This indicates the grade level at which your test performance is comparable.
4. **Cognitive Skills Quotient (CSQ)**: A measure of your critical thinking and problem-solving abilities, providing further insight into your academic potential.

What does it all mean? Each high school you've applied to will use your score report to determine whether you meet their entrance criteria. While some schools may focus on overall scores, others may give particular weight to specific sections. Schools know that the HSPT is just one part of your overall application. They also consider other factors like teacher recommendations, essays, and interviews.

After your test is scored, STS sends the results to the schools you listed during registration. Each school will then compare your performance to their specific requirements to decide if you qualify for admission.

The HSPT scoring system is built to give you every opportunity to shine. With no penalties for wrong answers, you can focus on doing your best without fear of losing points. The key is to approach the test with a calm, confident mindset and a solid strategy for tackling each section.

How to Prepare for the HSPT

Preparing for the High School Placement Test (HSPT) doesn't have to feel overwhelming. With the right tools, strategies, and mindset, you can approach test day with confidence and poise. Here's how to make the most of your preparation journey.

Step 1: Start Here—Understand the Test

By reading this chapter, you've already taken the first step toward success. Familiarizing yourself with the format, sections, and types of questions on the HSPT gives you a clear advantage. Knowledge is power, and understanding what to expect lays the foundation for effective preparation.

Step 2: Target Your Study Efforts

Once you know the details of the exam, dive into the instructional chapters focused on different specific areas. Whether it's brushing up on math concepts, honing your vocabulary, or practicing logical reasoning, this book has you covered with targeted lessons, tips, and practice questions. Improvement takes time. Celebrate small victories as you master challenging concepts.

Step 3: Measure Your Growth with Practice Tests

After spending focused time studying, take the practice HSPT tests in Chapter 7 . This will help you gauge how much progress you've made and refine your strategy further. Use them as an opportunity to boost your confidence by seeing tangible results from your hard work.

This test prep book is your ultimate guide for sharpening your skills, building confidence, and practicing the HSPT format. While it can't replace everything you've learned in school, it's an invaluable tool for:

- Reviewing key concepts.
- Practicing exam-specific question types.
- Developing effective test-taking strategies.

If there's something you didn't fully grasp in school, this book offers a chance to revisit those topics and gain a clearer understanding.

By committing to the steps above, you're equipping yourself with the knowledge, skills, and confidence needed to excel on the HSPT. Remember, this journey isn't just about the test—it's about opening doors to exciting opportunities in your high school education and beyond. Stay positive, stay focused, and you've got this.

Chapter Two: Reading Comprehension

Ever wondered how some students seem to know exactly what a passage means? In this chapter, you'll unlock the secrets to reading comprehension success.

Types of Reading Comprehension Questions

Reading comprehension questions on tests like the HSPT are designed to assess your ability to understand, analyze, and interpret written material. While these questions may seem tricky at first glance, understanding the different types of questions you will face can give you the confidence and strategy you need to excel. Here's a breakdown of the key types of reading comprehension questions you'll encounter, along with strategies to tackle them effectively.

1. Identifying Specific Facts or Details

The most straightforward of reading comprehension questions, these require you to pinpoint a specific piece of information from the passage. This could be a date, a name, a number, or a particular description. The goal here is to locate facts that directly support the main idea of the passage.

Example:

- **Passage**: "In 2020, the population of Paris reached 2.1 million people."
- **Question**: What was the population of Paris in 2020?
- **Answer**: 2.1 million.

Remember, these questions are designed to test your ability to find factual details, so accuracy is key. Avoid distractions like filler phrases and irrelevant information not asked for by the question.

2. Identifying the Main Idea

The main idea question asks you to determine the central theme or overall message of the passage. This could be an argument the author is making, an overarching opinion, or a key point they want you to take away.

Example:

- **Passage**: "Coach Susan Richmond's arrival drastically improved the team's performance. Under her leadership, the team increased their batting average by 50%, proving that her coaching skills were the key to their success."
- **Question**: What is the main idea of the passage?
- **Answer**: Coach Susan Richmond's leadership improved the team's performance.

Main idea questions will not necessarily have exact quotes to match, so you'll need to think about the passage as a whole and what the author wants to convey.

3. Making Inferences

Inference questions test your ability to read between the lines. They ask you to draw conclusions based on the information presented, even if that information isn't explicitly stated in the text. This is often the trickiest type because it requires a deep level of understanding.

Example:

- **Passage**: "The team's batting average rose by 50% after Coach Susan Richmond was hired, but the team's previous coach had a much less successful track record."
- **Question**: What can you infer from this passage?
- **Answer**: The previous coach was not as effective as Coach Richmond.

An inference question doesn't ask you for a guess or opinion—it asks you to deduce logically evidence in the passage.

4. Defining Vocabulary Words

Vocabulary questions ask you to determine the meaning of a word as it is used in the context of the passage. While you may not always know the exact definition of a word, you can often figure it out based on how it's used in the sentence or paragraph.

Example:

- **Passage**: "The team's performance improved markedly under Coach Richmond's supervision. Her meticulous attention to detail was the key to their success."
- **Question**: What does the word 'meticulous' mean?
- **Answer**: Very careful and precise.

Vocabulary questions are less about memorizing definitions and more about understanding how words function in the text. Context is your best friend here.

Practice Passage 1: Using the Four Question Types

The Evolution of the Telephone

The telephone is one of the most important inventions in modern history. It allows people to communicate over long distances, a convenience that has shaped the way we live and work today. However, the telephone as we know it today is very different from its predecessors.

The idea of the telephone was first conceived by Alexander Graham Bell, a Scottish-born inventor. In 1876, Bell successfully patented his version of the telephone, which transmitted voice signals over electrical wires. Bell's first telephone was quite rudimentary and had many limitations. It required a large amount of equipment to work, and the sound quality was poor compared to what we have now.

In the years following Bell's invention, other inventors worked to improve the telephone. Elisha Gray, an American electrical engineer, was one of the most notable. He is often credited with inventing a similar device, which led to a lengthy legal battle over the patent. Despite the conflict, Gray's contributions helped make future advancements in telecommunication.

By the 20th century, the telephone had undergone significant changes. One major improvement was the introduction of the rotary dial, which made it much easier to place calls. Later, the introduction of the touch-tone system replaced the rotary dial with push buttons, allowing for faster and more efficient dialing.

The next major leap came with the advent of mobile phones in the 1980s. These portable devices allowed users to make calls without being tied to a landline. Mobile phones became smaller, more affordable, and much more powerful as technology advanced, and by the 21st century, smartphones were introduced. These devices were no longer limited to voice calls but could send text messages, browse the internet, and run a variety of applications.

Today, telephones are an integral part of daily life, constantly evolving to meet the needs of modern society.

Questions

1. **Who was the first person to patent the telephone?**

    a. Elisha Gray
    b. Alexander Graham Bell
    c. Steve Jobs
    d. Thomas Edison

2. **What was a major improvement made to the telephone in the early 20th century?**

    a. The invention of the mobile phone.
    b. The introduction of the touch-tone system.
    c. The addition of the internet browser.
    d. The development of smartphone apps.

3. **The purpose of this passage is most likely to:**

    a. Explain the challenges faced by early telephone inventors.
    b. Outline the history and evolution of the telephone.
    c. Persuade readers to adopt mobile phones.
    d. Compare the telephone to other communication devices.

4. **Read the following sentence from the third paragraph:** "Despite the conflict, Gray's contributions helped make future advancements in telecommunication."

    As used in the sentence, the word *advancements* most nearly means:

    a. improvements
    b. setbacks
    c. failures
    d. repetitions

Answer Key and Explanation

1. **b. Alexander Graham Bell**

    - Bell was the first person to successfully patent the telephone in 1876.

2. **b. The introduction of the touch-tone system**

    - The touch-tone system replaced the rotary dial and made dialing more efficient.

3. **b. Outline the history and evolution of the telephone**

- The passage provides a timeline and key advancements in the development of the telephone.

4. **a. improvements**

- The word "advancements" refers to progress or improvements, which were made as a result of Gray's contributions.

Detail and Main Idea Questions

When approaching reading comprehension questions, you'll encounter two main types of questions that focus on the core information of the passage: **detail questions** and **main idea questions**. Both types of questions are direct, asking you to pull information right from the text. However, each one requires a different kind of thinking.

Detail or Fact Questions

Detail or fact questions are usually the easiest to answer because they simply require you to find a specific piece of information mentioned in the passage.

The key to mastering detail questions is recognizing that the information is always clearly stated somewhere in the passage. Your job is to find it. The challenge often lies in the fact that the answer choices may seem quite similar. For instance, two answer choices might mention almost identical facts, but one will be more precise or match the passage's wording exactly. Here's a strategy to tackle these questions effectively:

1. **Read the questions first**: Before diving into the passage, glance at the questions. This helps you focus on what details to look for as you read. Knowing the specific information you need to find will save you time and reduce confusion.
2. **Stay focused on the text**: Once you've identified what to look for, go back

to the passage and find the exact detail that answers the question. You don't need to memorize everything in the passage—just concentrate on finding the key detail relevant to each question.
3. **Beware of similar choices**: Some wrong answers might be very close to the correct one, so always double-check the wording. The correct answer will be the one that matches the passage precisely.

Main Idea Questions

Main idea questions, on the other hand, ask you to identify the general focus or the "umbrella" concept of the passage. This type of question is about understanding the passage's big picture rather than specific details.

The main idea is what the entire passage is mostly about. It's like the central theme that ties everything together. A passage about the evolution of the bicycle might have a main idea that summarizes the development of bicycles over time, while a passage about a specific bicycle model would have a narrower focus. The main idea often helps you understand the overall purpose of the passage.

In **main idea questions**, there are two possibilities:

1. **Stated Main Idea**: Sometimes, the main idea is directly expressed in the passage, often in the **first or last sentence**. This is often called the **topic sentence**. If the passage starts with "The history of the bicycle spans over two centuries and involves many technological innovations," that sentence likely summarizes the main idea of the passage.
2. **Implied Main Idea**: In other cases, the main idea is implied throughout the passage and isn't directly stated. To answer a main idea question, you'll need to **synthesize** all the details and ideas in the passage to determine what they collectively convey. Look for a summary that brings together all the key ideas. Ask yourself, "What does this passage ultimately want me to know?"

Sometimes, the wrong answers to main idea questions are specific facts or details that appear in the passage. These may seem appealing, but they don't hold the passage together like the main idea does. Always ask yourself, "Can this answer serve as a net that covers the entire passage?" If it's a specific detail, it's probably not the correct answer.

Practice Passage 2: Detail and Main Idea Questions

Good nutrition is essential for maintaining a healthy lifestyle. A balanced diet includes a variety of foods from different food groups: fruits, vegetables, proteins, grains, and dairy. Each food group provides specific nutrients that the body needs to function properly. Fruits and vegetables are rich in vitamins and minerals that help support the immune system, while proteins are vital for muscle repair and growth. Grains, such as whole wheat and brown rice, provide energy and help with digestion. Dairy products, like milk and cheese, supply calcium for strong bones and teeth.

It is also important to eat in moderation. Overeating, even healthy foods, can lead to weight gain and other health issues. Portion control is key, and it's important to be mindful of serving sizes. Additionally, drinking plenty of water throughout the day helps maintain hydration and supports bodily functions. While occasional treats are fine, it is important to make healthy choices most of the time to keep your body nourished and energized.

1. **Which of the following would be the best title for this passage?**

    a. The Importance of Moderation in Eating
    b. A Guide to Healthy Eating
    c. Eating for Energy
    d. Benefits of Drinking Water

2. **What is the primary function of proteins in the diet?**

    a. To support the immune system.
    b. To repair and grow muscles.
    c. To provide hydration.
    d. To support digestion.

3. **Which of the following best describes the main idea of the passage?**

   a. A balanced diet includes food from all food groups.
   b. Water is the most important part of a healthy diet.
   c. Eating treats occasionally is important for a healthy diet.
   d. Moderation and healthy food choices are essential for good health.

4. **According to the passage, which of the following is a good source of calcium?**

   a. Brown rice
   b. Whole wheat
   c. Milk and cheese
   d. Fruits and vegetables

Answers and Explanations

1. **b. A Guide to Healthy Eating**
   This is a **main idea question**. The passage provides a comprehensive overview of healthy eating habits, discussing various food groups and the importance of a balanced diet. Answer *b* is the best option because it captures the general theme of the passage. Answers *a*, *c*, and *d* focus on narrower aspects, like moderation or specific foods, but do not cover the entire scope of healthy eating.

2. **b. To repair and grow muscles**
   This is a **detail question**. The passage specifically mentions that "proteins are vital for muscle repair and growth." This makes *b* the correct answer. The other options refer to functions of different food groups mentioned in the passage, but proteins are primarily linked to muscle repair.

3. **d. Moderation and healthy food choices are essential for good health.**
   This is a **main idea question**. The passage emphasizes that making healthy food choices and eating in moderation are key components of maintaining good health. This option best captures the overall theme of the passage. Answers *a*, *b*, and *c* focus on particular details, such as food groups or water, but do not encompass the entire passage.

4. **c. Milk and cheese**
   This is a **detail question**. The passage clearly states that "dairy products, like milk and cheese, supply calcium for strong bones and teeth." Therefore, *c* is the correct choice. The other options do not provide calcium, as the passage links dairy specifically to this function.

Inference and Vocabulary Questions

When preparing for reading comprehension tests, understanding **inference** and **vocabulary questions** challenge your ability to think beyond the surface level and require you to analyze the deeper meaning in a passage. They engage critical reading skills, and mastering them can significantly enhance your test performance.

Inference Questions

Inference questions are designed to test your ability to understand ideas that are not directly stated but suggested or implied in the text. In other words, they require you to "read between the lines." These questions often feel like a puzzle, and just like a detective solving a case, you must carefully analyze the passage for clues.

Let's say you read a passage about a character walking through a dark, quiet forest and feeling nervous, with occasional noises that startle them. An inference question might ask: *What can we infer about how the character feels?* While the passage never explicitly says, "The character feels scared," you can infer it based on the clues—such as the darkness of the forest, the silence, and the character's reaction to the noises. These are all clues pointing to fear or anxiety.

How to approach inference questions:

1. **Identify Clues:** Look for words, phrases, or actions that hint at emotions, attitudes, or conclusions. These may not be directly stated, but they provide valuable context.
2. **Ask Yourself Why:** After reading the passage, ask yourself why the author

included certain details. What feelings or thoughts might these details suggest? Your goal is to form a conclusion that logically fits with the passage, supported by evidence within it.
3. **Test Your Answer:** Once you've made an inference, check it against the passage. Can you find specific evidence that backs up your conclusion? If not, it's time to reconsider.

By practicing these steps, you will develop the ability to identify subtle hints and make educated inferences that are rooted in the passage itself—not based on assumptions or outside knowledge.

Vocabulary Questions

Vocabulary questions assess your ability to understand the meaning of unfamiliar words by using their context. The context is the surrounding information—words, phrases, or sentences—that help explain the unfamiliar word's meaning.

For example, consider the following sentence:

The teacher's explanation of the concept was so convoluted that the students were left bewildered.

From the context, you can infer that "bewildered" means confused or puzzled. Even if you've never encountered the word before, the surrounding details (like "so convoluted") provide clues to its meaning.

How to approach vocabulary questions:

1. **Use Context Clues:** Focus on the sentences or phrases around the unfamiliar word. These often contain hints to its meaning. Ask yourself: *What is the general idea of the sentence? How does this word fit within it?*
2. **Substitute a Nonsense Word:** A trick to test if you understand the context is to replace the unknown word with a nonsense word. If the sentence still makes sense, you've likely understood the intended meaning of the word.
3. **Break Down the Word:** If the word is complex, try breaking it down into recognizable parts—prefixes, suffixes, or roots. If you encounter the word

"prejudice," you might recognize "pre-" (before) and "judice" (judgment), helping you deduce that it means making a judgment before knowing all the facts.

4. **Don't Rely on Prior Knowledge:** It's tempting to rely on your previous knowledge of a word's meaning, but in test situations, a word may have multiple meanings based on its context. Always ensure your interpretation aligns with how it is used in the passage.

Consider the word "taut" in the following sentence:
The rope was pulled taut, ready for the climber to scale the rock face.

From the context, you can conclude that "taut" means tight or stretched. If you confused it with "taunt," which means to tease, you'd be misinterpreting the word.

Practice Passage 3: Inference and Vocabulary Questions

The Earth orbits the Sun in a tilted position, which causes the different seasons throughout the year. In the Northern Hemisphere, the tilt of the Earth results in longer days and warmer temperatures during the summer months. Conversely, when the Northern Hemisphere is tilted away from the Sun, it experiences winter, with shorter days and cooler temperatures. The Southern Hemisphere experiences the opposite, with summer occurring when the Northern Hemisphere is in winter, and vice versa.

1. According to the passage, when it is summer in the Northern Hemisphere, it is _____ in the Southern Hemisphere.

    a. spring
    b. summer
    c. autumn
    d. winter

2. From the passage, it can be inferred that the Earth's tilt is responsible for:

    a. The difference between day and night.

b. The change of seasons.
   c. The Earth's distance from the Sun.
   d. The length of days during each season.

3. The word "orbit," as it is used in the passage, most closely means:

   a. A path or course.
   b. The angle at which Earth is tilted.
   c. A circular motion.
   d. A point of maximum distance from the Sun.

Answers and Explanations for Practice Passage

1. d. winter

This is an inference question. The passage clearly states that when it is summer in the Northern Hemisphere, it is winter in the Southern Hemisphere. This can be inferred based on the Earth's tilt and how the northern and southern hemispheres experience opposite seasons.

2. b. The change of seasons.

This is an inference question as well. The passage explains that the tilt of the Earth causes the different seasons. When the Earth is tilted towards or away from the Sun, it leads to longer or shorter days and the transition between summer and winter. This change in seasons is directly linked to the Earth's tilt.

3. a. A path or course.

The word "orbit" refers to the path the Earth follows around the Sun. The context of the passage suggests that the Earth moves in an elliptical orbit, influencing the seasons. "Orbit" does not refer to the angle of tilt or the distance from the Sun but rather to the course the Earth takes around it.

We've explored the essential strategies and techniques to tackle reading comprehension questions effectively. Focusing on key question types—such as detail, main idea, inference, and vocabulary—can enhance your ability to identify critical information, draw logical conclusions, and determine word meanings from context. Practicing these skills will help you navigate passages more confidently and accurately, ensuring a thorough understanding of the material.

Chapter Three: Vocabulary

Vocabulary is the cornerstone of your communication toolkit. Your ability to express ideas clearly and precisely isn't just a nice-to-have; it's a must-have skill for high school and beyond. That's why HSPT has vocabulary questions front and center. In this chapter, we will walk you through the commonly tested vocabulary questions and make vocabulary one of your greatest strengths.

Kinds of Vocabulary Questions

The HSPT assesses vocabulary through two primary formats:

1. **Synonyms and Antonyms**

    These questions test your ability to identify words that have similar (*synonyms*) or opposite (*antonyms*) meanings. This format evaluates your capacity to make precise distinctions between words and their relationships. **Tip:** If the word is unfamiliar, analyze its structure—prefixes, roots, and suffixes often hold valuable clues.

2. **Context Clues**

    These questions provide a word within a sentence or passage and ask you to determine its meaning based on how it is used. By carefully examining the surrounding words and overall context, you can uncover the word's intended meaning.

Tip: Look for comparisons, contrasts, or examples in the sentence—they often provide hints to the correct answer.

Synonym Questions

Synonym questions ask you to identify a word that has the same or nearly the same meaning as the given word. While the concept is straightforward, the challenge lies in recognizing less familiar words and their subtle nuances.

For example:

- A synonym of *quick* is *fast*.
- A synonym of *happy* is *joyful*.

However, on the HSPT, you're more likely to encounter advanced words where understanding prefixes, suffixes, and roots becomes critical.

There is no way you are going to memorize all synonyms present in the dictionary. So, you have to be strategic about answering these questions. Some tips that we recommend:

- **Analyze Word Parts:** Breaking down the word into its components can reveal its meaning. For instance, in the word *corroborated*, the prefix *co-* means "together," suggesting an association with confirming or verifying.
- **Eliminate Incorrect Choices:** Even if you are unsure of a word's exact meaning, eliminating options that clearly do not fit the context can narrow your choices and improve your odds.
- **Consider Word Associations:** Sometimes, the sound or structure of a word can remind you of a related term. For example, *substantial* shares its root with *substance*, indicating something significant or weighty.

Synonyms Practice

Let's apply these strategies to some sample synonym questions:

1. **A partial answer**

    a. identifiable
    b. incomplete
    c. visible
    d. enhanced

Answer: b. Partial means incomplete. The key clue is the root part, which indicates only a portion of something.

2. **Substantial advice**

    a. inconclusive
    b. weighty
    c. proven
    d. alleged

Answer: b. Substantial advice is weighty. The root substance hints at something with depth or significance.

3. **Corroborated the statement**

    a. confirmed
    b. negated
    c. denied
    d. challenged

Answer: a. Corroborated means confirmed. The prefix co- suggests working together, aligning with the idea of verification.

4. **Ambiguous questions**

    a. a. meaningless
    b. b. difficult
    c. c. simple
    d. d. vague

Answer: d. Ambiguous means vague or uncertain. The prefix ambi- means "both," suggesting a question open to more than one interpretation.

Antonym Questions

Antonym questions ask you to identify a word that means the opposite of the given word. While synonyms focus on similarity, antonyms demand precision in recognizing contrast. For instance:

- The antonym of *hot* is *cold*.
- The antonym of *success* is *failure*.

Straightforward, right? But the HSPT likes to make things more challenging by presenting complex words and including synonyms as decoys in the answer choices. Staying focused on finding the *opposite* is essential to avoid falling for these traps.

We believe antonyms are a tad bit more difficult than synonyms. That's why you need to be very careful when answering these questions. Here are some tips to keep in mind:

- **Highlight the Key Word:** If the test directions allow, circle or underline the word *antonym* in the question prompt to remind yourself you're looking for the opposite meaning. This simple step can help you avoid confusing antonyms with synonyms.
- **Analyze Word Structure:** Similar to synonym questions, prefixes, roots, and suffixes can provide critical hints. For example:
- The prefix *in-* in *inadvertently* suggests "not," which gives a clue about the word's meaning.
- **Eliminate Synonyms:** Test makers often include synonyms of the given word as tempting wrong answers. Cross out choices that are too similar to the word in question and focus on identifying the true opposite.
- **Think Contextually:** If the word seems unfamiliar, consider a context where you may have encountered it before. Associating the word with a scenario or phrase can help you deduce its meaning and find its antonym.

Antonym Practice

Let's explore some sample antonym questions to see these strategies in use:

5. Zealous pursuit

   a. envious
   b. eager
   c. idle
   d. comical

Answer: b. The word zealous means eager or enthusiastic, so its opposite is idle, meaning inactive or unmotivated. Avoid confusing zealous with jealous—similar sounds, but different meanings.

6. Inadvertently left

   a. a. mistakenly
   b. b. purposely
   c. c. cautiously
   d. d. carefully

Answer: b. Inadvertently means by mistake, so the opposite is purposely. The prefix in- here suggests "not," reinforcing that inadvertent actions are unintentional.

7. Exorbitant prices

   a. expensive
   b. unexpected
   c. reasonable
   d. outrageous

Answer: c. Exorbitant means excessively high, so the opposite is reasonable. The prefix ex- (meaning "out of") hints at something going beyond limits, like "out of orbit."

8. Compatible workers

a. comfortable
b. competitive
c. harmonious
d. experienced

Answer: b. The opposite of compatible (meaning harmonious) is competitive. Here, all the answer choices include the prefix com-, but competitive stands out as the contrast.

9. Belligerent attitude

a. hostile
b. reasonable
c. instinctive
d. ungracious

Answer: b. Belligerent means warlike or aggressive, so the opposite is reasonable. The root belli- (from Latin, meaning "war") is key to understanding the word's meaning.

Context Questions

Context refers to the words, phrases, or sentences surrounding an unfamiliar term. These hints can include:

- Synonyms or antonyms in the same sentence.
- Comparisons or contrasts that clarify the meaning.
- Clues from the overall tone or subject of the passage.

For instance, consider the sentence:

"The children were ecstatic when they heard they were going to the amusement park." Even if you don't know the exact meaning of *ecstatic*, you can infer it means something like *very happy* because of the situation described.

Context questions are often more manageable because the test gives you a built-in "helper" in the form of the surrounding text. Here are some strategies to get them right:

- **Look for Clues in the Sentence:** Pay attention to keywords or phrases that define, explain, or relate to the unfamiliar word. Words like *because*, *but*, or *however* can signal relationships or contrasts that provide valuable insights.
- **Rely on the Process of Elimination:** If you're unsure of the answer, rule out choices that clearly don't fit the context. By narrowing your options, you increase your odds of selecting the right answer.
- **Focus on the Sentence's Tone and Theme:** Consider the overall message of the sentence or paragraph. Is the tone positive or negative? Is the context formal or casual? Understanding this can help guide you to the correct choice.
- **Watch for Trap Words:** Some answer choices may sound similar to the target word but don't fit the sentence. Stay focused on the context rather than being distracted by surface-level similarities.

Context Practice in Action

Let's apply these strategies to a few sample questions.

10. **The clerks in the store were appalled by the angry customer's wild and uncontrolled behavior.**

    a. horrified
    b. amused
    c. surprised
    d. dismayed

Answer: a. The words wild and uncontrolled suggest a reaction of horror rather than amusement or mild surprise. The surrounding description makes it clear.

11. **Despite the fact that he appeared to have financial resources, the client claimed to be destitute.**

    a. wealthy
    b. ambitious
    c. solvent
    d. impoverished

Answer: d. The word despite signals contrast. While financial resources imply wealth, destitute must mean the opposite—impoverished.

12. **Though she was distraught over the disappearance of her child, the woman was calm enough to give the officer her description.**

    a. punished
    b. distracted
    c. composed
    d. anguished

Answer: d. The contrast introduced by though suggests opposites. Distraught (upset) contrasts with calm, so anguished is the best fit.

13. **The unrepentant embezzler expressed no remorse for his actions.**

    a. sympathy
    b. regret
    c. reward
    d. complacency

Answer: b. The key words no and unrepentant indicate a lack of regret. Even if you're unfamiliar with remorse, the sentence context clarifies its meaning.

14. **Professor Washington was a very _____ man known for his reputation as a scholar.**

a. stubborn
b. erudite
c. illiterate
d. disciplined

Answer: b. The words professor and scholar point toward erudite, meaning highly educated. Even if you don't know erudite, the other choices don't fit the sentence's positive tone.

15. His _____ was demonstrated by his willingness to donate large amounts of money to worthy causes.

a. honesty
b. loyalty
c. selfishness
d. altruism

Answer: d. The key phrase large amounts of money to worthy causes provides a definition of altruism—selfless generosity.

Word Parts

The building blocks of words—prefixes, roots, and suffixes carry specific meanings that can guide you in deciphering unfamiliar words. While the HSPT doesn't test word parts directly, mastering them can make you more confident in tackling vocabulary questions.

Word parts are the components that make up a word:

- **Roots:** The core meaning of the word. Example: *port* (to carry).
- **Prefixes:** Added before the root to modify its meaning. Example: *re-* (again) in *replay*.
- **Suffixes:** Added after the root to change the word's use or meaning. Example: *-able* (capable of) in *readable*.

Here are some helpful techniques that will help you master word parts:

- **Connect New Words to Familiar Ones:** When you encounter a new word, think of others you already know with the same root, prefix, or suffix. For example, if you know *predict* means to say something before it happens, you can infer that *prelude* means something that comes before.
- **Pay Attention to Common Prefixes and Suffixes:**

    o **Common Prefixes:**

    - *un-* (not): unhappy, unclear
    - *re-* (again): rewrite, retell
    - *pre-* (before): pretest, preview

    o **Common Suffixes:**

    - *-able* (capable of): readable, fixable
    - *-less* (without): fearless, careless
    - *-tion* (the act of): celebration, action

- **Visualize Root Meanings:** Roots often carry vivid imagery. For instance, the root *scrib-* means to write. Think of *scribble*, *describe*, or *manuscript*. These connections help the word stick in your memory.
- **Use Context as a Safety Net:** If you're unsure about a word part, lean on the context clues in the sentence to verify your guess.

Word Part Practice

Let's test your knowledge! Circle the word or phrase below that best matches the underlined portion of the word.

16. proactive

    a. after
    b. forward
    c. toward

d. behind

17. recession

a. against
b. see
c. under
d. back

18. contemporary

a. with
b. over
c. apart
d. time

19. etymology

a. state of
b. prior to
c. study of
d. quality of

20. vandalize

a. to make happen
b. to stop
c. to fill
d. to continue

Answers and Explanations

16.   b. Forward

Pro- means forward. Think of words like *propel* (to push forward).

17. d. Back

Re- often means back or again. For example, *recall* (to bring back).

18. a. With

Con- means with or together, as in *congregation* (people gathering together).

19. c. Study of

The suffix *-ology* means the study of, as in *biology* (study of life) or *psychology* (study of the mind).

20. a. To make happen

The suffix *-ize* often means to make something happen. For example, *realize* (to make real) or *scandalize* (to cause a scandal).

A Comprehensive List of Word Parts

Below is an expanded table of common word elements that frequently appear in vocabulary tests and everyday usage. Spend a few minutes daily reviewing these elements to strengthen your ability to decode unfamiliar words with ease.

WORD ELEMENT	MEANING	EXAMPLES
ama	love	amateur, amorous
ambi	both	ambivalent, ambidextrous
aud	hear	audition, auditory
belli	war	belligerent, bellicose
bene	good	benefactor, benevolent
bio	life	biology, biography
cid/cis	cut	homicide, scissors
cogn/gno	know	recognize, incognito
contra/counter	against	contradict, counterbalance

curr/curs	run	current, cursive
dic/dict	speak, say	dictate, predict
duc/duct	lead	conduct, introduce
flu/flux	flow	fluid, fluctuate
fort	strength	fortify, fortress
gress	to go	progress, regress
in/im	not, in	incomplete, implant
ject	throw	inject, reject
luc/lux/lum	light	lucid, illuminate
mal	bad	malnourished, malicious
neo	new	neophyte, neonatal
omni	all	omnivorous, omniscient
path	feeling, disease	empathy, pathology
pel/puls	push	impulse, propeller
phobia	fear	claustrophobia, arachnophobia
pro	forward	project, propel
pseudo	false	pseudonym, pseudoscience
rog	ask	interrogate, arrogant
scrib/script	write	describe, manuscript
spec/spic	look, see	spectator, conspicuous
sub	under	subjugate, submarine
super	over	superfluous, supernatural
temp	time	temporary, contemporary
trans	across	transport, transparent
un	not, opposite	uncoordinated, unreal
vid/vis	see	visible, envision
viv/vit	live	vivid, vital

Confusing Words

Vocabulary tests and everyday usage can be tricky due to words that are easily confused. Mastering these distinctions can greatly enhance your test-taking abilities.

WORD PAIR	MEANING
accept / except	accept: to receive willingly / except: to exclude or leave out
affect / effect	affect: to influence / effect: a result
allusion / illusion	allusion: an indirect reference / illusion: a misconception
alternately / alternatively	alternately: in turn, one after the other / alternatively: one or the other
beside / besides	beside: next to / besides: also
capital / capitol	capital: seat of government or wealth / capitol: legislative building
cite / site	cite: to quote or formally recognize / site: location
complement / compliment	complement: to complete / compliment: to say something flattering
concurrent / consecutive	concurrent: happening simultaneously / consecutive: happening successively
connote / denote	connote: to imply or suggest / denote: to indicate or refer specifically
continuous / continual	continuous: without interruption / continual: occurring from time to time
council / counsel	council: a decision-making group / counsel: advice or guidance
discreet / discrete	discreet: prudent or modest / discrete: separate or distinct
disinterested / uninterested	disinterested: unbiased or impartial / uninterested: indifferent
elicit / illicit	elicit: to draw out / illicit: unlawful
emigrate / immigrate	emigrate: to move from / immigrate: to move to
farther / further	farther: more distant / further: to a greater extent or additionally
few / less	few: small in number, countable / less: small in amount, uncountable
figuratively / literally	figuratively: metaphorically / literally: exactly or actually
flaunt / flout	flaunt: to show off / flout: to show contempt
foreword / forward	foreword: introductory note / forward: toward the front or to send on
historic / historical	historic: important in history / historical: related to the past

ingenious / ingenuous	ingenious: clever / ingenuous: naive or guileless
lightening / lightning	lightening: to make lighter / lightning: electrical flashes in a storm
oral / verbal	oral: pertaining to the mouth / verbal: pertaining to language
passed / past	passed: past tense of "pass" / past: time gone by
persecute / prosecute	persecute: to oppress / prosecute: to bring legal action
principal / principle	principal: a high-ranking person / principle: a fundamental rule
stationary / stationery	stationary: unmoving / stationery: writing materials

More Vocabulary Practice

This practice set has been crafted to sharpen your skills while keeping it fun and insightful. Dive in, challenge yourself, and see how well you fare with synonyms, antonyms, and context-based word puzzles.

Find the Synonym

Circle the word that means the same or nearly the same as the underlined word:

1. amateur athlete

    a. professional
    b. successful
    c. unrivaled
    d. former

2. convivial company

    a. lively
    b. dull
    c. tiresome
    d. dreary

3. conspicuous behavior

   a. secret
   b. outrageous
   c. visible
   d. boorish

4. lucid opinions

   a. clear
   b. strong
   c. hazy
   d. heartfelt

5. meticulous record-keeping

   a. dishonest
   b. casual
   c. painstaking
   d. careless

6. traveling incognito

   a. a. unrecognized
   b. alone
   c. by night
   d. publicly

7. incisive reporting

   a. mild
   b. sharp
   c. dangerous
   d. insightful

8. tactful comments

   a. a. rude

b. b. pleasant
c. c. complimentary
d. d. sociable

Find the Antonym

Circle the word that is most nearly opposite in meaning to the underlined word:

9. superficial wounds

    a. life-threatening
    b. bloody
    c. severe
    d. shallow

10. impulsive actions

    a. cautious
    b. imprudent
    c. courageous
    d. cowardly

Context-Based Synonyms

Using the context, choose the word that means the same or nearly the same as the underlined word:

11. Though he had little time, the student took copious notes in preparation for the test.

    a. limited
    b. plentiful
    c. illegible
    d. careless

12. Though flexible about homework, the teacher was adamant that papers be in on time.

    a. liberal
    b. casual
    c. strict
    d. pliable

13. After the party, the condition of the room was deplorable.

    a. regrettable
    b. pristine
    c. festive
    d. tidy

Fill in the Blank

Choose the word that best completes the following sentences:

14. Her position as a(n) _____ teacher took her all over the city.

    a. primary
    b. secondary
    c. itinerant
    d. permanent

15. Despite her promise to stay in touch, she remained _____ and difficult to locate.

    a. steadfast
    b. stubborn
    c. dishonest
    d. elusive

Breaking Down Word Parts

Choose the word or phrase closest in meaning to the underlined part of the word:

16. universe

    a. one
    b. three
    c. under
    d. opposite

17. re-entry

    a. back
    b. push
    c. against
    d. forward

18. benefit

    a. bad
    b. suitable
    c. beauty
    d. good

19. education

    a. something like
    b. state of
    c. to increase
    d. unlike

20. urbanite

    a. resident of
    b. relating to
    c. that which is
    d. possessing

Answers and Explanations

1. **a. professional**: "Amateur" means non-professional; the opposite is "professional".
2. **a. lively**: "Convivial" means friendly and lively.
3. **c. visible**: "Conspicuous" refers to something noticeable or easily seen.
4. **a. clear**: "Lucid" means easy to understand or transparent in meaning.
5. **c. painstaking**: "Meticulous" implies extreme attention to detail, synonymous with "painstaking."
6. **a. unrecognized**: "Incognito" refers to being in disguise or not recognized.
7. **b. sharp**: "Incisive" means clear and direct, often cutting to the core of an issue.
8. **b. pleasant**: "Tactful" refers to being sensitive and thoughtful in interactions.
9. **d. shallow**: "Superficial" means on the surface, so its opposite would be "deep" or "severe"
10. **a. cautious**: "Impulsive" describes acting without thought; the opposite is "cautious"
11. **b. plentiful**: "Copious" means abundant or in large quantities.
12. **c. strict**: "Adamant" refers to being unyielding or strict.
13. **a. regrettable**: "Deplorable" means deserving strong condemnation or regret.
14. **c. itinerant**: Refers to traveling or moving from place to place.
15. **d. elusive**: Describes someone difficult to pin down or locate.
16. **a. one**: The prefix "uni-" means one, as in "universe."
17. **a. back**: The prefix "re-" means again or back.
18. **d. good**: "Benefit" means an advantage or good thing.
19. **b. state of**: The suffix "-tion" often denotes a state or condition.
20. **a. resident of**: "Urbanite" refers to someone who resides in a city.

Chapter Four: Language Skills

Grammar doesn't have to be a guessing game. In this chapter, you'll learn how to master HSPT language skills, from sentence structure to punctuation.

What HSPT Usage Questions Are Like

HSPT usage questions test your ability to spot errors in sentences. The task is straightforward:

1. Read a set of sentences.
2. Find the one that contains an error in grammar or usage.
3. If no errors exist, select the option that says **"No mistakes."**

Sounds simple enough, right? The trick lies in paying close attention to details like verb tenses, pronouns, and sentence structure. These questions evaluate how well you understand the mechanics of language, and they reward those who are sharp-eyed and quick-thinking.

Let's take a look at a typical HSPT usage question:

Question 1:

   a. Will you join me for dinner?
   b. Molly had chose not to attend.
   c. I am wearing my sister's coat.
   d. No mistakes.

Answer:

The error is in **b**. The correct verb form is **had chosen**, not **had chose**.

These questions challenge you to:

- **Identify errors in sentence construction**: Incomplete or awkward sentence structures are often hiding in plain sight.
- **Spot incorrect verb usage**: Pay attention to tense consistency—like "has went" instead of the correct "has gone."
- **Catch pronoun errors**: For example, "Him and I went to the store" should be "He and I went to the store."

To tackle these questions effectively, you'll need a solid grasp of grammar basics. But don't worry! The more you practice, the easier it will get to notice these subtle slip-ups.

Sentences

Complete Sentences

Sentences are the building blocks of writing, and their effectiveness lies in their completeness. A complete sentence delivers a full thought. It has two essential components:

- **A subject**: the "who" or "what" the sentence is about.
- **A verb**: the action or state of being.

Here's an example:

- **Complete Sentence**: *We saw the tornado approaching.*
  This has both a subject (*we*) and a verb (*saw*), and it expresses a full thought.

In contrast:

- **Fragment**: *When we saw the tornado approaching.*
  This leaves the reader hanging. What happened when we saw the tornado? It's an incomplete thought.

Spotting Sentence Fragments

Fragments are like unfinished puzzles—they're missing a critical piece. Sometimes, a fragment appears to have a subject or verb but lacks the necessary structure to stand alone.

Take these examples:

- *The dog walking down the street.*
  At first glance, it seems like a sentence, but it's not. Why? The word *walking* acts as an adjective here, not a verb.

To fix it:

- **Complete Sentence**: *The dog was walking down the street.*
  Adding the helping verb (*was*) makes all the difference

Subordinating Conjunctions:

Words like *when*, *because*, *after*, and *where* are tricky. They transform a perfectly good sentence into a fragment when added without completing the thought.

For example:

- *When I opened the box.*
  This isn't complete—you're left wondering, *What happened when the box was opened?*

Fixed version:

- **Complete Sentence**: *When I opened the box, I found a treasure inside.*

Run-on Sentences

Run-on sentences are the opposite of fragments—they cram too much together without proper punctuation. They often occur when two or more sentences are joined incorrectly.

Here are some examples of run-ons and how to fix them:

1. **Run-on**: *We went to the beach, we had a good time.*

   o **Fixed**: *We went to the beach. We had a good time.*

2. **Run-on**: *Emily wanted to stay home with her new hamster, her mom said she had to go to school.*

   o **Fixed**: *Emily wanted to stay home with her new hamster. Her mom said she had to go to school.*

The golden rule? If it feels like too much is crammed into one sentence, it probably is. Break it down.

If you are trying to crack this type of questions, here are some advice:

- **Check for a Subject and Verb**: Every sentence needs these. If one is missing, it's incomplete.
- **Beware of -ing Words**: Words ending in *-ing* need a helping verb to form a complete sentence (e.g., *is walking*, *was running*).
- **Look Out for Conjunctions**: Subordinating conjunctions often turn complete sentences into fragments.
- **Avoid the Comma Splice**: If you're connecting two complete thoughts, use a period or a semicolon—not just a comma.

Mastering Verbs

Verbs are the heartbeat of a sentence—they tell us what's happening, when it's happening, and who's doing it. Let's explore the essentials of verbs: **Subject-Verb Agreement** and **Verb Tense**.

Subject-Verb Agreement

Subject-verb agreement might sound like a grammar buzzword, but it's simply about harmony between the subject and the verb. Here's the golden rule:

- **A singular subject takes a singular verb.**
- **A plural subject takes a plural verb.**

When in doubt, test it! Let's use the verbs *speak* and *do* to illustrate:

- **One person speaks. One person does.**
- **Two people speak. Two people do.**

This quick test ensures your verbs match the subject perfectly.

Some of the examples might be a little more complicated than others. Such as:

1. **Compound Subjects**:

    o *The cat and the dog play outside.* (Plural subject = plural verb)
    o *Neither the cat nor the dog plays outside.* (Singular subject closer to the verb = singular verb)

2. **Indefinite Pronouns**:

    Words like *everyone* or *nobody* might seem plural but are singular.

    o *Everyone enjoys the movie.*
    o *Nobody likes cold coffee.*

Verb Tense

Verb tense places your reader in the timeline of your story. There are three main tenses:

- **Present Tense**: Action happening now.
- **Past Tense**: Action that has already happened.
- **Future Tense**: Action that will happen.

Let's see how tenses shape a scene:

- Present Tense : *Horace opens the door and glances around cautiously. He sees signs of danger everywhere.*
- Past Tense: *Horace opened the door and glanced around cautiously. He saw signs of danger everywhere*
- Future Tense: *Horace will open the door and glance around cautiously. He will see signs of danger everywhere.*

Sometimes, changing tenses is necessary to clarify timing. For instance: *The game warden sees the fish that you caught.*

- *Sees* (present tense) indicates the action happening now.
- *Caught* (past tense) shows that the fish was caught earlier.

This careful shift helps pinpoint when each action occurred without confusion.

The HSPT often tests your ability to spot subject-verb agreement errors and tense inconsistencies. When approaching these questions:

1. Identify the subject and check if the verb matches in number.
2. Review the tense and ensure it aligns with the sentence's timeline.

Clear Sentences

Clear sentences are the backbone of effective communication. On the HSPT, questions that test your ability to spot the clearest sentence challenge not only your grammar skills but also your ability to convey ideas in a straightforward, logical way.

Here's how you can tackle this type of questions:

Accuracy First: Always start by checking if the facts in the sentence are accurate. Even the most elegantly written option is incorrect if it misrepresents the information. Example:

- Incorrect: Robert discovered a movie being filmed at 9:00 p.m.
- Correct: At 8:25 p.m., Robert found MGM filming a movie.

Tip: Don't get swayed by fancy phrasing—focus on factual correctness first.

Plain English, Please: The best sentence is straightforward and easy to understand without rereading. Avoid sentences overloaded with complex phrasing or jargon. Example:

- Unclear: At 8:25 p.m., while ambling along Main Street, Robert stumbled upon a cinematic venture orchestrated by MGM.
- Clear: At 8:25 p.m., Robert turned the corner on Main Street and found MGM filming a movie.

Tip: Ask yourself, "Would I say it this way in a conversation?" If the answer is no, there's likely a simpler option.

Logical Order: Information should be presented in a sequence that makes sense, usually chronological or cause-and-effect. Scrambled ideas confuse readers and reduce clarity.

Example:

- Confusing: Robert saw MGM filming a movie after he turned the corner, at 8:25 p.m. on Main Street.
- Clear: At 8:25 p.m., Robert turned the corner on Main Street and found MGM filming a movie.

Tip: Think of the sentence as a story—what happened first, and what followed?

Active Verbs Create Impact: Active voice brings energy and focus to a sentence, while passive voice can make it feel distant or unnecessarily formal. Example:

- Passive: A movie was being filmed by MGM on Main Street.
- Active: MGM was filming a movie on Main Street.

Tip: Look for verbs that directly connect the subject to the action. Active verbs make your writing more engaging and conversational.

When evaluating sentence clarity, follow these steps:

1. Read each sentence aloud. If it feels clunky or confusing, it's likely not the clearest option.
2. Spot the active verbs. Favor sentences where the subject actively performs the action.
3. Check for logical flow. Does the sentence lead the reader smoothly from one idea to the next?

HSPT Punctuation and Capitalization

Mastering punctuation and capitalization is essential for success on the HSPT. These questions test your ability to spot errors in sentences and, just as importantly, to recognize when a sentence is error-free.

Capitalization:

Capitalization serves as a guidepost in writing, highlighting beginnings, proper nouns, and important titles. Missteps in capitalization can confuse readers or obscure meaning, so it's important to follow the rules carefully. Here are the core capitalization rules for you to follow in your HSPT exam:

1. **Start Strong:**

    o   Always capitalize the first word of a sentence.
    o   If the sentence begins with a number, spell the number out.
    o   Example: *Twenty students attended the seminar.*

2. **The Pronoun "I" Always Stands Tall**

    o   The personal pronoun *I* is always capitalized, no matter its placement in a sentence.
    o   Example: *She said, "I will attend the meeting."*

3. **Quotations: Full vs. Partial**

    o   Capitalize the first word in a complete quotation.

        ▪ Example: *He asked, "What time is the meeting?"*

    o   Do not capitalize the first word in a partial quotation.

        ▪ Example: *He referred to her as "the best artist" in the gallery.*

4. **Proper Nouns and Adjectives**

    o   Always capitalize names, titles, specific places, organizations, and proper adjectives.
    o   Examples:

        ▪ *Names*: Sarah Johnson, Abraham Lincoln
        ▪ *Places*: Mississippi River, Grand Canyon
        ▪ *Adjectives*: French cuisine, Victorian architecture

Examples in Action: Consider these sentences:

- Incorrect: *in april, we visited the Grand canyon.*
- Correct: *In April, we visited the Grand Canyon.*

Punctuation

Punctuation is the structure that keeps sentences clear and coherent. Whether it's marking the end of a sentence or showing possession, proper punctuation is essential for accurate writing.

Periods

Here's where to use periods:

1. **Ending Sentences**

   o Use a period to end declarative sentences and indirect questions.
   o Example: *She is attending the conference.*

2. **Abbreviations**

   o Place periods after abbreviations unless the abbreviation is an acronym.
   - Example: *Dr., a.m., Inc.*
   - Acronyms: *NASA, UNICEF*

   o If a sentence ends with an abbreviation, use only one period.
   - Example: *He brought food, drinks, utensils, etc.*

3. **After Initials in Names**

   o Use a period after initials in personal names.
   o Example: *J.K. Rowling, W.E.B. Du Bois*

Examples in Action: Consider this sentence:

- Incorrect: *Dr Smith is meeting us at 10 a.m*
- Correct: *Dr. Smith is meeting us at 10 a.m.*

Sample Question:

Find the sentence that has a mistake in capitalization or punctuation. If there are no mistakes, mark choice d.

   a. *We visited Glacier National Park last summer.*
   b. *Dr Wilson examined the patient on Thursday.*
   c. *She asked, "who will bring the refreshments?"*
   d. *No mistakes.*

Answer: The correct answer is **c**. The word *who* should be capitalized as it begins a quotation:

- Corrected: *She asked, "Who will bring the refreshments?"*

Commas

When used correctly, commas can transform complex ideas into easily digestible sentences. Misplacing a comma, however, can distort meaning or create confusion. Let's look at the core rules for comma usage and how they guide clarity.

1. **Before Coordinating Conjunctions in Compound Sentences**

    o Use a comma before *and, but, or, for, nor, so,* and *yet* when they connect two independent clauses (complete sentences).
    o Example: *I wanted to join the club, but I missed the application deadline.*

2. **Separating Items in a Series**

    o Place commas between three or more items in a list.
    o Example: *We packed sandwiches, fruit, water, and sunscreen for the picnic.*

3. **Between Multiple Adjectives Modifying the Same Noun**

    o Use commas between adjectives that describe the same noun, but not before the noun itself.

- Example: *The tall, graceful, strong horse won the race.*

4. **After Introductory Words, Phrases, or Clauses**

    - Add a comma to separate introductory elements from the main sentence.
    - Examples:

        - *Certainly, I understand your point.*
        - *Walking through the park, she spotted a rare bird.*
        - *When the storm ended, the sun broke through the clouds.*

5. **In Names, Dates, and Addresses**

    - Use commas after elements of names, dates, and addresses.
    - Examples:

        - *Martin Luther King, Jr. delivered a historic speech.*
        - *They arrived on March 15, 2023, to celebrate.*
        - *Send the letter to 123 Elm Street, Springfield, Illinois.*

6. **Setting Off Contrasting Elements**

    - Use commas to separate contrasting ideas or phrases.
    - Example: *I need focus, not distractions, to finish this project.*

7. **Appositives: Providing Clarity**

    - Use commas to set off appositives—phrases that rename or clarify a noun.
    - Example: *My sister, a talented musician, performed at the recital.*

Commas are not just about grammar—they can dramatically alter the meaning of a sentence:

- *My sister Diane, John, Carey, Melissa, and I went to the fair.* (Five people are attending, and Diane is not clarified as my sister.)

- *My sister, Diane, John, Carey, Melissa, and I went to the fair.* (Six people are attending, and Diane is clarified as my sister.)

The careful placement of commas ensures that your intended meaning is clear to your audience.

Apostrophes

Apostrophes pack a powerful punch, whether they're used for contractions or showing possession. Misusing apostrophes can lead to confusion, so understanding their rules is vital.

1. **Contractions: Shortening Words**

    o Apostrophes replace omitted letters in contractions.
    o Examples:

     - *Do not* becomes *don't.*
     - *You are* becomes *you're.*

2. **Showing Possession**

    o Apostrophes indicate ownership. The placement of the apostrophe depends on whether the noun is singular or plural.

     - **Singular Nouns:** Add 's.
       - Example: *The dog's leash is missing.*
     - **Plural Nouns Ending in S:** Add only an apostrophe.
       - Example: *The girls' uniforms are clean.*
     - **Plural Nouns Not Ending in S:** Add 's.
       - Example: *The children's playground is newly built.*

Here are some of the common mistakes that you might make in your HSPT exam:

- Misplacing apostrophes:

    o Incorrect: *The dogs bone is buried in the yard.*

o Correct: *The dog's bone is buried in the yard.*

- Confusing plurals with possessives:
    - Incorrect: *The cats are sleeping in the sun's warmth.*
    - Correct: *The cat's are sleeping in the sun's warmth.* (singular cat)
    - Correct: *The cats' are sleeping in the sun's warmth.* (multiple cats)

Sample Question: Commas

Question: Identify the sentence with a comma error.

a. *She packed sandwiches, juice, and fruit for lunch.*
b. *After the movie, we grabbed coffee and dessert.*
c. *The noisy, crowded classroom distracted me.*
d. *They went to Paris, and visited the Eiffel Tower.*

Answer:

The correct answer is **d**. The comma before *and* is unnecessary because it does not connect two independent clauses. The corrected sentence: *They went to Paris and visited the Eiffel Tower.*

Sample Question: Apostrophes

Question: Identify the sentence with an apostrophe error.

a. *The teacher's instructions were clear.*
b. *The students' projects were outstanding.*
c. *Its a beautiful day outside.*
d. *The women's team won the match.*

Answer:

The correct answer is **c**. The contraction *Its* should be *It's*.

HSPT Spelling

In the HSPT spelling section, you'll encounter three sentences labeled **a, b,** and **c**. One sentence may contain a misspelled word, or none at all. Your task is to identify the error—or choose **d: No mistakes.** To excel, you'll need a strong grasp of foundational spelling rules, an awareness of tricky exceptions, and strategies for spotting mistakes.

Know the Rules: Understanding the fundamentals of English spelling can provide a solid foundation for tackling errors. Here are some key rules to remember:

- **"I before E, except after C"**

    o Example: *piece, receive*
    o Exception: Words like *neighbor* and *weigh* where the "ei" sounds like "ay."

- **Silent Letters**

    o *gh* can be silent or represent a unique sound.
    o Examples: *enough, night*

- **Doubling Consonants**

    o Double the final consonant when adding endings to words with short vowel sounds.
    o Examples: *shop → shopping, forget → forgettable*

- **Dropping the Final "E"**

    o Drop the "e" before adding "-ing" unless it changes the word's meaning.
    o Example: *hope → hoping*

- **Prefixes and Suffixes**

    o Prefixes and suffixes generally don't alter the root word's spelling.
    o Examples: *project → proactive, play → playful*

Watch for Exceptions: English is full of irregularities, making it crucial to recognize when rules don't apply. Words like *scissors* or *business* don't follow conventional patterns but remain common on spelling tests.

To get your HSPT spelling answers right, follow the following techniques.

1. **Sound It Out:** Break the word into syllables and listen for clues. For instance:

    - Long vowels are often followed by single consonants (*total*).
    - Short vowels are typically followed by double consonants (*dribble*).

2. **Use Auditory Clues:** Pronounce words as they're spelled, not as they're spoken in casual conversation.

    - Examples:

        o Say *Wed-nes-day* instead of *Wensdy*.
        o Say *lis-ten* instead of *lissen*.

3. **Break It Down:** Look for familiar parts like prefixes, roots, or suffixes. These elements often remain consistent:

    - **Uninhabitable** = un- + in- + habit + -able.

4. **Build a Spelling Toolkit:** Practice actively with spelling lists.

    o **Make Flashcards:** Focus on words you find challenging.
    o **Highlight Tricky Elements:** Emphasize silent letters (*psychology*) or irregular patterns (*debt*).
    o **Group Words by Similarity:** Study words with shared rules or patterns together.

Sample Question: Let's review an example:

Question: Identify the sentence with a misspelled word.

   a. *The exhibition showcased student artworks from every grade.*

b. *The coach berated me for arriving late to practice.*
c. *I felt embarassed when I dropped my tray in the cafeteria.*
d. *No mistakes.*

Answer: The correct choice is **c**. The correct spelling is *embarrassed*.

HSPT Composition

The HSPT Composition section evaluates your ability to recognize and construct effective sentences and paragraphs. Beyond correcting grammatical errors, this section challenges you to identify clarity, coherence, and logical flow.

This section tests your understanding of:

- Logical paragraph development.
- Effective sentence structure.
- Organization and coherence in writing.

You'll encounter questions that ask you to:

- Identify topic sentences or controlling ideas.
- Choose the best word or phrase to connect ideas.
- Spot irrelevant sentences or misplaced ideas.
- Recognize patterns of organization that enhance clarity.

Through these tasks, the HSPT ensures you can analyze and produce well-structured compositions—a skill critical for academic success.

Crafting Effective Paragraphs

An outstanding paragraph has three key characteristics:

- **A Controlling Idea:**

Every paragraph begins with a topic sentence that introduces the main idea. For example, in the well-written paragraph about bats:

"There are many myths about bats that need to be dispelled if we are to come to appreciate these fascinating creatures."

This sentence clearly states the focus, setting the stage for supporting details.

- **Logical Organization:**

The structure of a paragraph should guide the reader smoothly from the main idea to supporting examples or evidence. In the bat paragraph, the writer dispels myths one by one, creating a logical flow of information.

- **Coherent Sentences:**

Sentences should connect seamlessly, without redundancy or awkward phrasing. Compare the polished paragraph with the scrambled or poorly constructed versions—it's easy to see how clarity impacts readability.

Recognizing Strong Composition:

Here's what sets strong writing apart:

- **Clarity and Precision:**
- Clear writing avoids vague or ambiguous statements. For instance:

    o Weak: *Bats are kind of like mice but not really.*
    o Strong: *Although bats resemble mice superficially, their anatomy and behavior reveal key differences.*

- **Relevance:**

    o Every sentence should contribute to the main idea. An irrelevant statement, such as *"You can learn many interesting facts from an encyclopedia,"* distracts from the paragraph's purpose.

- **Effective Transitions:**
  - Transitional phrases like *"for example,"* *"however,"* and *"in contrast"* ensure ideas flow logically. Without them, writing feels disjointed.

Composition Strategies for Success

Now you might be wondering what type of questions you might face in this section. Here are common composition question types and tips on how to approach them:

1. **Choosing the Best Transition:**

   - Look for a word or phrase that logically connects two ideas.
   - Example: *Bats use echolocation to navigate. (____), they are not blind.*
     - Answer: *However* (to contrast the myth with reality).

1. **Spotting the Irrelevant Sentence:**

   - Identify the sentence that doesn't align with the paragraph's main idea.
   - Example: In a paragraph about bat myths, a sentence about bird migration would be irrelevant.

2. **Reorganizing Sentences:**

   - Ensure the paragraph follows a logical sequence, starting with a clear topic sentence and ending with a conclusion.

3. **Selecting the Most Clear Expression:**

   - Choose the phrasing that is straightforward and grammatically correct.
   - Example:

- **Weak:** *Bats aren't blind, and they got a radar system.*
- **Strong:** *Bats are not blind; they use a highly developed radar system to navigate.*

4. **Placing a Sentence in the Right Spot:**

    o Read the paragraph and determine where the sentence fits best to maintain logical flow.

5. **Choosing the Right Essay Topic:**

    o Select a topic that aligns with the prompt's purpose and allows for a clear, focused discussion.

The composition section is all about practice. But you can utilize these strategies to get ahead and find answers faster

- Think Like an Editor: Imagine you're polishing a draft for publication. Does every sentence add value? Does the paragraph flow smoothly from one idea to the next?
- Look for Patterns of Organization: Common structures include:

    o **Chronological Order:** Events described in the order they occur.
    o **Cause and Effect:** Explaining reasons and results.
    o **Compare and Contrast:** Highlighting similarities and differences.

- Practice Paragraph Revisions: Rewriting scrambled or poorly constructed paragraphs (like the examples about bats) helps develop an intuitive sense of flow and clarity.
- Use Context Clues: Pay attention to surrounding sentences when tackling questions about sentence placement or transitions.

Examples of Well-Developed and Incoherent Paragraphs

Paragraph #1

Topic Sentence:
The monarch butterfly is one of nature's most fascinating migratory species.

Supporting Details:

Every fall, these delicate creatures travel thousands of miles from Canada to Mexico, guided by an internal compass that scientists are still trying to understand. Along the way, they face numerous challenges, such as unpredictable weather, dwindling food supplies, and habitat destruction. Despite these obstacles, monarchs persevere, relying on milkweed plants for sustenance and as a place to lay their eggs. This incredible journey demonstrates not only the resilience of these butterflies but also the intricate interconnectedness of ecosystems, as their survival depends on the conservation efforts of humans and the environment they traverse.

This paragraph has a clear topic sentence, logical progression of ideas, and relevant supporting details, all of which align with the main idea of the monarch butterfly's migration.

Paragraph #2

Topic Sentence:
The monarch butterfly is one of nature's most fascinating migratory species.

Details (Scrambled and Irrelevant):

They eat milkweed plants, which are very important for their survival. You can find information about butterflies in books or on websites about animals. The weather can be bad sometimes. Monarchs travel thousands of miles from Canada to Mexico. Humans can help monarchs by planting milkweed. Migration is a long process. Some monarchs don't make it because of predators or lack of food.

This paragraph is disorganized, with ideas scattered randomly and some sentences irrelevant to the topic sentence. For instance, the mention of finding information in books does not contribute to understanding the monarch butterfly's migration. The lack of logical flow makes it hard to follow and less effective in conveying the main idea.

Chapter Five: Verbal and Nonverbal Reasoning

Think you can spot patterns and analogies? In this chapter, we guide you through verbal and non-verbal reasoning questions to test your logic skills.

The Verbal Skills section of the HSPT includes five question types:

- Verbal Analogies
- Synonyms
- Logic
- Verbal Classification
- Antonyms.

While Synonyms and Antonyms are discussed in Chapter 7, this chapter will jump into Verbal Analogies, Logic, and Verbal Classification.

Verbal Analogies

Verbal analogies are designed to test your ability to recognize relationships between words and apply them logically. Understanding analogies helps you develop critical thinking skills, as they require you to discern how two words are connected and use that connection to complete another set. These questions evaluate your ability to reason, spot patterns, and make logical connections.

In a typical analogy question, you are given two words that have a specific relationship. You'll then need to select the pair of words from the answer choices that share a similar relationship. Here's how it works:

Example 1:

Aspirin is to headache as bandage is to:

   a. injection
   b. sprain
   c. wound
   d. welt

Answer: c. wound

This is a classic example of a "use or function" analogy. Aspirin is used to treat a headache, and similarly, a bandage is used to treat a wound. While sprains, injections, and welts are related to injury or health, none of them fit the functional role that a bandage has in relation to a wound as effectively as choice c. In this case, understanding the functional relationship is key to solving the problem.

Verbal analogies are among the most challenging sections of the HSPT, requiring both a deep understanding of word meanings and the ability to identify the relationships between them. However, with the right approach, you can get the job done. Here's how you can systematically and confidently tackle verbal analogy questions:

1. **Look at the Literal Meaning of the Words:** The foundation of any analogy is understanding the literal meaning of each word involved. If you don't know what a word means, it's impossible to identify how it fits into a relationship with another word. The key here is wide reading—expose yourself to a variety of texts, from textbooks to magazines, and even everyday instructions or product descriptions. The more you read, the more likely you are to encounter new words and understand their meanings.

   When you come across a word you're unfamiliar with, take a moment to look it up. This habit will expand your vocabulary and sharpen your ability to understand word meanings in context. Additionally, remember to apply the skills you've learned about synonyms, antonyms, and word roots. Understanding word parts will give you clues about meanings, especially when encountering complex words.

2. **Make Up a Sentence:** Once you've grasped the meanings of the words, the next step is to figure out the relationship between them. A helpful technique is to make up a sentence that expresses the relationship between the first pair of words. This method forces you to articulate the connection, which can clarify the type of analogy at play.

Take the following analogy:

Aspirin is to headache as bandage is to:

    a. injection
    b. sprain
    c. wound
    d. welt

Step 1: Start by creating a sentence that reflects the relationship:

"Aspirin is used to treat a headache." Now, try plugging each answer choice into a similar sentence:

- "A bandage is used to treat an injection?" Nope. This doesn't make sense, so option a is eliminated.
- "A bandage is used to treat a sprain?" This is possible, but not the best match. Bandages can treat sprains, but the relationship isn't as clear as with the next option.
- "A bandage is used to treat a wound?" Yes! This is a perfect fit. A bandage is typically used to treat a wound, just like aspirin is used to treat a headache.
- "A bandage is used to treat a welt?" While a bandage might help with a welt, it's not the primary treatment, making this option less accurate.

Result: The correct answer is "wound," as it aligns best with the functional relationship in the first set.

3. **Look at the Exact Relationship Between the Words:** After understanding the meanings of the words, focus on the type of relationship they share. Some common types of relationships include:

   - **Function or Use**: One word describes the purpose or function of another (e.g., aspirin to headache, bandage to wound).
   - **Cause and Effect**: One word causes or results in the other (e.g., rain to wet, sun to heat).
   - **Part to Whole**: One word is a part of the other (e.g., finger to hand, petal to flower).
   - **Synonym/Antonym**: The two words share a similar or opposite meaning (e.g., happy to joyful, hot to cold).

   In your analogy practice, pay close attention to what type of relationship the words are expressing. Identifying the relationship will help you quickly rule out incorrect answers and find the one that matches.

4. **Remember That a Word May Have Several Meanings:** Words often have multiple meanings, so be mindful of context. The word "shoulder" can refer to a part of the body or the side of a road. The meaning of the word will depend on the context in which it appears. When working through analogies, always ensure you understand the context in which the word is being used. Making up a sentence can help clarify the intended meaning.
5. **Watch Your Time:** The analogy section of the HSPT is known for being one of the most difficult, so it's essential to manage your time wisely. Don't waste too much time on one question. If you're stuck, skip the question and return to it later. Consider tackling the analogy questions first during your practice sessions to get a feel for how you can approach them efficiently.
6. **Practice, Practice, Practice:** Ultimately, the best way to excel at verbal analogies is through consistent practice. The more you practice, the more you'll become familiar with the different types of relationships between words. Make use of sample analogy questions and answer explanations to refine your skills. As you practice, try to categorize the types of analogies you encounter, as recognizing these patterns will help you quickly identify the relationship in future questions.

Practice Analogy Questions & Answers

1. **Groom is to wedding as lawyer is to:**
   a. crime
   b. accident
   c. trial
   d. client

Answer: c. trial

Explanation: This is a **part-to-whole** analogy. A groom is a part of a wedding, just as a lawyer is a part of a trial. This relationship reflects how one word (groom) fits within the broader context of the other word (wedding). While other options might sound plausible, "trial" is the best fit because a lawyer is directly involved in a trial, much like a groom is at the center of a wedding.

2. **Mouse is to mammal as pickup is to:**

   a. car
   b. wheel
   c. truck
   d. driver

Answer: c. truck

Explanation: This analogy is based on **classification**. A mouse is a type of mammal, just as a pickup is a type of truck. The key here is recognizing that both mouse and mammal, as well as pickup and truck, are categories where one is a subset of the other.

3. **Gale is to breeze as terror is to:**

   a. uneasiness
   b. scream
   c. intimidation
   d. irritation

Answer: a. uneasiness

Explanation: This is a **proportion or degree** analogy. A gale is an intense wind, while a breeze is a mild one. Similarly, terror is an extreme form of fear, and uneasiness is a milder version of fear. This relationship helps you recognize how two concepts are related by their intensity or degree.

4. **Weeping is to grief as tantrum is to:**

    a. fit
    b. kicking
    c. loudness
    d. rage

Answer: d. rage

Explanation: This is a **cause-and-effect** analogy. Weeping is a response to grief, just as a tantrum is often a response to rage. It's important to note that a tantrum is caused by strong emotions, similar to how weeping is caused by grief.

5. **Love is to hate as optimism is to:**

    a. depression
    b. meanness
    c. pessimism
    d. realism

Answer: c. pessimism

Explanation: This is a **similarity or difference** analogy. Love and hate are opposite emotions, just as optimism and pessimism are opposite attitudes. Recognizing the opposing nature of the words in the analogy is key to solving this one.

6. **Teeth are to mouth as brick is to:**

    a. kiln
    b. wall
    c. clay
    d. masonry

Answer: b. wall

Explanation: This analogy relies on a **part-to-whole** or **whole-to-part** relationship. Teeth are part of the mouth, just as bricks are part of a wall. The relationship expresses how one word is a piece of a larger whole.

7. **Halloween is to witch as summer is to:**

    a. vacation
    b. season
    c. winter
    d. time

Answer: a. vacation

Explanation: This is an analogy based on **strong association**. Halloween is strongly associated with witches, just as summer is strongly associated with vacations. While "season" might seem like a reasonable answer, the stronger association here is with "vacation"

8. **Enraged is to irritated as broken is to:**

    a. smashed
    b. damaged
    c. cracked
    d. irreparable

Answer: c. cracked

Explanation: This is another **proportion or degree** analogy. To be enraged is to be intensely angry, while irritated is a milder form of anger. Similarly, to be broken is to be severely damaged, while cracked is a less severe form of damage. The difference in intensity or degree is what ties these pairs together.

9. **Explore is to discovery as exercise is to:**

    a. aerobics

    b. sports
    c. running
    d. fitness

Answer: d. fitness

Explanation: This is a **cause-and-effect** analogy. Exploring leads to discovery, just as exercise leads to fitness. The connection is direct: exercise is something you do to achieve a state of fitness, just as exploring results in a discovery.

10. **Organ is to heart as dog is to:**

    a. canine
    b. poodle
    c. breed
    d. mammal

Answer: b. poodle

Explanation: This is a **classification** analogy. An organ is a type of body part, and the heart is a specific example of an organ. Similarly, a poodle is a type of dog, which makes it the correct answer. Note that the order of the words is crucial—just like the heart is a type of organ, a poodle is a type of dog.

HSPT Number Series

Number Series questions on the HSPT test your ability to identify patterns and reason with sequences. These questions challenge you to think critically, analyze relationships between numbers, and predict the next terms in a series. Though they might seem daunting at first, they become manageable—and even enjoyable—with practice and a structured approach. Let's explore how to confidently tackle Number Series questions.

Number Series questions present a sequence of numbers with a specific pattern or rule governing their progression. Your task is to uncover the underlying logic and determine the next numbers in the series. These questions measure your ability to recognize patterns, test hypotheses, and apply logical reasoning—all essential skills for academic success.

For example:

1. Look at this series: 37 35 33 31 29 27 25…

What two numbers should come next?

    a. 24 23
    b. 24 22
    c. 23 21
    d. 22 20

The correct answer is **c. 23, 21**. The pattern involves subtracting 2 from each preceding number (37 → 35 → 33, and so on). By continuing this sequence, we get 25 → 23 → 21.

If you are still having confusion around this, here are some tips for decoding number series questions:

1. **Identify the Pattern:** Start by examining the sequence for obvious patterns. Common types of patterns include:

    - **Arithmetic sequences** (adding or subtracting a constant value).
    - **Geometric sequences** (multiplying or dividing by a constant value).
    - **Alternating patterns** (e.g., every second or third number follows a distinct rule).
    - **Repetitive elements** (e.g., numbers that appear at regular intervals).

2. **Read the Series Aloud:** If the pattern isn't immediately clear, try pronouncing the sequence in your head. Hearing the rhythm or cadence of the numbers can often reveal the pattern.

    For instance, in the series **10, 12, 50, 15, 17, 50, 20…**, saying the numbers aloud while ignoring the repetitive "50" helps isolate the main sequence: 10 → 12 → 15 → 17 → 20.

3. **Break It Down into Smaller Parts:** If the sequence is complex, focus on every second or third number to see if smaller, simpler patterns emerge. Complex series often combine multiple rules, so isolating individual components can make them easier to solve.
4. **Look for Repetition:** Some sequences include repeated numbers or symbols that seem random. These repeated elements may serve as placeholders or separators and are not part of the actual pattern.
5. **Test Hypotheses:** After spotting a potential pattern, test it with the given numbers to ensure consistency. Predict the next numbers based on your hypothesis and confirm they fit the sequence.

Now, that you have an understanding on how to answer these questions, let's work through a more complex example:

2. Look at this series: 10 12 50 15 17 50 20...

What two numbers should come next?

   a. 50 21
   b. 21 50
   c. 50 22
   d. 22 50

Solution:

- Notice the repetitive "50." Treat it as a separator and focus on the remaining numbers: **10, 12, 15, 17, 20.**
- The sequence alternates between adding 2 and adding 3:

    o 10 → 12 (+2)
    o 12 → 15 (+3)
    o 15 → 17 (+2)
    o 17 → 20 (+3)

- Continuing this pattern, the next number is **20 + 2 = 22**.
- Reinsert the repetitive "50" to complete the series: **22, 50.** The correct answer is **d. 22, 50.**

Number Series questions are not just about math—they test your ability to think logically and adapt quickly. Each question challenges you to spot nuances and apply rules efficiently, which is why practice is crucial. By working through various examples and reviewing explanations, you'll build familiarity with different types of patterns and gain confidence in solving even the trickiest sequences.

Geometric and Non Geometric Comparison

Geometric and Non Geometric Comparison questions are unique elements of the HSPT that test your ability to analyze relationships between shapes, patterns, or values. While they may seem visually or conceptually distinct, the approaches to solving these types of questions are strikingly similar. Success in these sections requires sharp observation, logical reasoning, and an understanding of comparative analysis. With the right strategies, you can tackle these problems confidently and efficiently.

These questions are designed to assess your reasoning skills by presenting items that must be compared in terms of size, shading, length, or mathematical values. Here's how they are generally categorized:

1. **Geometric Comparison**

   These questions involve comparing visual elements, such as shapes or figures. For instance, you might need to determine which figure is larger, more shaded, or longer.

   Sample Question:
   Examine (A), (B), and (C) and find the best answer.

   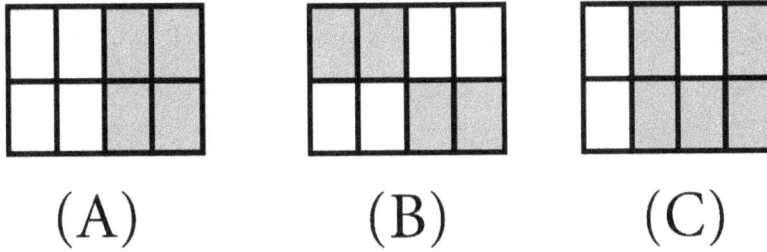

- (A) is more shaded than (B).
- (B) is more shaded than (C).
- (C) is more shaded than (A).
- (A) and (C) are equally shaded.

Answer: The correct answer is **(C)**. A quick comparison of the figures reveals that C is more shaded than A or B.

2. Non Geometric Comparison

These questions rely on numerical or symbolic comparisons. They challenge your ability to compute values and identify relationships between numbers.

Sample Question:
Examine (A), (B), and (C) and find the best answer.

- (A): 2+2+22+2+2
- (B): 14÷214÷2
- (C): 3 ┌(1+2)3 ┌(1+2)

Answer: First, evaluate each option:

- A=6A=6
- B=7B=7
- C=9C=9

Comparing the results, the correct answer is **(C) is greater than (A) or (B)**.

These questions are tricky and you need to really understand what the questions want from you. Here are some tips for tackling Geometric and Non Geometric Comparison Questions.

1. **Take It One Step at a Time:** Rushing through these problems can lead to errors. Focus on analyzing one element at a time—whether it's size, shading, or a numerical operation.
2. **Break Down Visual Elements:** For geometric questions, systematically compare each figure's size, shading, or dimensions. Look for measurable differences rather than relying on assumptions.
3. **Work Out the Math for Non Geometric Questions:** When comparing numerical expressions, calculate each option carefully. This ensures you identify the correct relationship between the values.
4. **Look for Overlapping Patterns:** Both question types may include overlapping logic. For example, shading intensity in geometric questions could parallel numerical values in non geometric ones, requiring the same systematic approach to analysis.
5. **Practice the Process:** The more you practice these types of questions, the faster and more accurately you'll recognize patterns. Create a mental checklist: observe, calculate, compare, and confirm

Practice Geometric and Non Geometric Comparison Question

Question 1: Identify the missing term in the sequence: EF_1G_2, HI_1J_3, KL_3M_4, NO_4P_5, _____.

a. QR_5S_6
b. QR_6S_7
c. RS_6T
d. PQ_6R_6

Question 2: Given the series: 78, 71, 64, 57, ..., what number should come next?

a. 43
b. 47
c. 48
d. 50

Question 3: Look at the series: 10, 5, 20, 10, 40, ..., what number should come next?

a. 10
b. 12
c. 20
d. 80

Question 4: Look at this series: II, III, V, VIII, XII, …, what Roman numeral should come next?

a. XVII
b. XX
c. XIV
d. XXII

Question 5: Given the series: 816, 408, ___, 102, 51, what number should fill the blank?

(A) ———————

(B) ————————

(C) —————————

(D) ——————

a. 26
b. 204
c. 214
d. 306

Question 6: Examine (A), (B), (C), and (D) and find the best answer:

- (A) is longer than (D).
- (B) and (D) are the same length.
- (A) is shorter than (B), but longer than (D).
- (A) + (D) is longer than (C).

Question 7: Examine the circles (A), (B), and (C) and determine the shading relationship:

- (A and C) are equally shaded.
- (A is more shaded than B, but less shaded than C).
- (A is less shaded than B, but more shaded than C).
- (Of the three, A is the least shaded).

Question 8: Examine (A), (B), and (C) and find the best answer:

```
X X X X        X X           X X
X X X          X X X X X     X X
X X                          X X X X
X                            X         X X
 (A)            (B)           (C)
```

- (A) and (C) have an equal number of x's.
- (C) has one more x than (A) has.
- (A) plus (B) equals (C).
- (A) plus (B) minus (C) equals 5.

Question 9: Examine (A), (B), and (C) and find the best answer:

(A) $\frac{1}{3}$ of 123

(B) $8^2 - 23$

(C) $9(9) - 40$

- (A), (B), and (C) are all equal.

- (A) plus (B) equals (C).
- (A) and (C) are equal, but (B) is less than both (A) or (C).
- (C) is one more than (A).

Question 10: Examine (A), (B), and (C) and find the best answer:

(A)   5% of 45

(B) $\frac{1}{6}$ of 12

(C)   10% of 22

- (A) and (C) are equal.
- (A) is less than (B).
- (C) is less than (A).
- (C) is greater than (A)

Answers and Explanation

Question 1: Correct Answer: (a)

The letter sequence follows simple alphabetical order, while the number sequence alternates in a repeating pattern: 1, 2, 2, 3, 3, 4, 4, 5, 5, 6. By breaking it down:

- Eliminate (c) and (d) because their letters are out of order.
- Eliminate (b) because the numbers don't fit the established sequence. Boom! The answer is **(a)**—a perfect balance of logic and order.

Question 2: Correct Answer: (d)

Starting at 78, each subsequent number is reduced by 7:

78 → 71 → 64 → 57 → 50.

The answer, (d), highlights the beauty of simplicity in math.

Question 3: Correct Answer: (c)

1. The first sequence doubles: 10 → 20 → 40.
2. The second sequence also doubles: 5 → 10 → 20.
3. Following this rhythm, the next number is **(c) 20**. The elegance of alternating patterns shines here!

Question 4: Correct Answer: (a)

Translating the series into Arabic numerals makes it crystal clear:

II (2) → III (3) → V (5) → VIII (8) → XII (12).

The progression adds 1, 2, 3, 4, and finally 5, leading to XVII (17). Pro tip: brush up on Roman numerals before test day—they're a game-changer!

Question 5: Correct Answer: (b)

Starting at 816, each number is halved:

816 → 408 → 204 → 102 → 51.

The key here is precision. Spotting the division pattern quickly leads you to (b).

Question 6: Line Correct Answer: (d)

After carefully testing each statement, it's clear that (A) plus (D) is longer than (C) is the only logical choice. Tip: don't rush—measure twice, decide once.

Question 7: Correct Answer: (c)

(A) has fewer shaded pieces than (B) but more than (C).

The answer is **(c)**, where observation meets strategy.

Question 8: Correct Answer: (b)

(A) = 10 X's, (B) = 7 X's, and (C) = 11 X's.

Testing the options leads to **(b)**, the logical choice. Counting correctly is your best friend here!

Question 9: Correct Answer: (a)

- (A): 1331 of 123 = 41
- (B): 82−23=4182−23=41
- (C): 9×9−40=419×9−40=41

  Clearly, all values match, making **(a)** the winner.

Question 10: Correct Answer: (c)

- (A): 5%5% of 45 = 2.25
- (B): 1661 of 12 = 2
- (C): 10%10% of 22 = 2.2

  Testing each reveals **(c)** as the standout answer.

Chapter Six: Math Skills

Math may seem intimidating, but with a clear approach, you can master any question. In this chapter, we are going to provide you all the tools you need to conquer the HSPT math section.

Word Problems

Word problems can feel like puzzles wrapped in math riddles, but they don't have to. When you know how to decode them, they're simply opportunities to combine language and numbers in creative ways. The biggest challenge in word problems is converting words into numbers and symbols. Luckily, there are key words and patterns that guide you.

Equals: The Core Connection

Key Words: *is, are, has*

When you see these words, they're signaling a mathematical equality. In other words, the left side equals the right side. For example:

- Bob **is** 18 years old → B= 18
- There **are** 7 nurses → N= 7
- This suborder **has** 5 families → F= 5

Translation tip: Anytime the problem mentions something that *"is"* or *"has"*, you're likely dealing with an equation.

Addition: Adding It All Up

Key Words: *sum, more, greater, older, total, altogether*

Additional problems are about putting things together. These keywords suggest relationships where one value builds on another:

- *The sum of two numbers is 10* → X+Y= 10
- *Karen has $5 more than Sam* → K= 5+S
- *Judi is 2 years older than Tony* → J= 2+T
- *The total of three numbers is 25* → A+B+C= 25

Pro tip: Words like "altogether" and "total" mean you're summing everything up, so look for all the pieces of the equation.

Subtraction: Finding the Difference

Key Words: *difference, less, fewer, younger, remain, left over*

Subtraction tells a story of taking something away or comparing differences:

- *The difference between two numbers is 17* → X−Y= 17
- *Mike has 5 fewer cats than twice the number Jan has* → M= 2J−5
- *Jay is 2 years younger than Brett* → J= B−2
- *After Carol ate 3 apples, how many apples remained?* → R= A−3

Pro tip: Subtraction often involves thinking in terms of what's "missing" or what's "left," so focus on what's taken away.

Multiplication: Amplifying the Numbers

Key Words: *of, product, times*

Multiplication problems emphasize scaling or repeated addition:

- *20% of the samples* → 0.20×S
- *Half of the bacteria* → ½ ×B
- *The product of two numbers is 12* → A×B= 12

Pro tip: When you see "of" or "times", think multiplication. Percentages always involve multiplying a decimal equivalent by the total.

Division: Splitting Things Up

Key Words: *per, half, divide, quotient, is divided by*

Division is all about distributing or breaking something into parts:

- *22 miles per gallon* → miles/22= gallons
- *22 is divided by 5* → ²⁄₅
- *One-half of 8* → 8/2

Pro tip: Words like "per" and "quotient" are your signal to divide, so keep an eye out for fractions or ratios.

Here are some tips that can help you solve these word problems quicker:

1. **Highlight Key Words**: Read the problem carefully and underline words like *"sum," "difference,"* or *"product"*—they're your clues.
2. **Simplify Sentences**: Break long sentences into smaller chunks to identify what's being asked.
3. **Sketch It Out**: Visual learners might benefit from diagrams or simple sketches to represent the problem.
4. **Solve Step-by-Step**: Focus on one part of the problem at a time. Isolate the math operation first, then solve.
5. **Double-Check**: Once you've solved, reread the problem to make sure your answer matches what's being asked.

Step-by-Step Problem Solving: Juan and the Jellybeans

Let's break down a more complex word problem to show how our translation rules come to life.

Problem:

Juan ate ⅓ of the jellybeans. Maria then ate ¾ of the remaining jellybeans, which left 10 jellybeans. How many jelly beans were there to begin with?

Choices:

   a. 60
   b. 80
   c. 90
   d. 120
   e. 140

Step 1: Translate Words into Math

1. Start by defining the unknown: Let J represent the total number of jellybeans.
2. Juan ate ⅓ of the jellybeans:

$$\text{Jellybeans eaten by Juan} = \frac{1}{3} \times J$$

3. The remaining jellybeans after Juan ate:

$$J - \frac{1}{3} \times J = \frac{2}{3} \times J$$

4. Maria ate ¾ of the remaining jellybeans:

$$\text{Jellybeans eaten by Maria} = \frac{3}{4} \times \frac{2}{3} \times J = \frac{1}{2} \times J$$

5. After Maria's feast, only ¼ of the ⅔ × J jelly beans were left:

$$\text{Remaining jellybeans} = \frac{1}{4} \times \frac{2}{3} \times J = \frac{1}{6} \times J$$

Step 2: Solve the Equation

The problem states that 10 jellybeans were left, meaning:

$$\frac{1}{6} \times J = 10$$

To find J, multiply both sides by 6:

$$J = 10 \times 6 = 60$$

Answer: a. 60

This problem demonstrates how essential it is to work step-by-step. Translating each action (eating, remaining, dividing) into a mathematical statement ensures accuracy. With this approach, even multi-step problems become less daunting. Now that we've mastered a complex problem, let's apply the translation method to more scenarios.

Practice Problems

1. **Joan's Shopping Trip**

    Joan started with $100.00 and returned home with $18.42. How much did she spend?

    Start with:

    ```
    Amount spent= Starting amount-Remaining amount
    ```

    Substituting values:

    ```
    100.00 −18.42= 81.58
    ```

    Answer: $81.58

2. Tutoring Center Capacity

Each of five tutors works six hours per day, tutoring three students per hour. How many students are seen daily?

- Start with:

$$\text{Students per tutor per day} = \text{Hours worked} \times \text{Students per hour}$$

$$\text{Total students} = 5 \times (6 \times 3)$$

$$= 5 \times 18 = 90$$

Answer: 90

3. Typing Speed

The office secretary types 80 words per minute. How long does it take to type 760 words?

- Start with:

$$\text{Time} = \text{Total words} \div \text{Words per minute}$$
$$760 \div 80 = 9.5 \text{ minutes}$$

Answer: 9½ minutes

4. Budget Request

Principal Wallace wants to buy:

- o $100 of RAM
- o 2 software programs at $350 each
- o 1 monitor at $249
- o 1 keyboard at $25

Total Cost:

$$100+(2\times350)+249+25= 1{,}074$$

Answer: $1,074

Number Names

In the HSPT math section, you're likely to encounter questions that ask you to convert written number names into digits or vice versa. These questions offer an excellent opportunity to rack up easy points, especially if you're familiar with the structure and place value system behind numbers. Knowing how to read and write number names confidently will help you breeze through these questions with ease.

Numbers are composed of digits, each representing different values depending on its position. This is the concept of place value, and mastering it is key to understanding how to write number names correctly.

For example, in the number **4,312.796:**

- The **4** is in the **thousands** place, representing **4,000**.
- The **3** is in the **hundreds** place, representing **300**.
- The **1** is in the **tens** place, representing **10**.
- The **2** is in the **ones** place, representing **2**.

To the right of the decimal point, the values represent fractional parts of a whole:

- The **7** is in the **tenths** place, representing **seven-tenths (0.7 or 7/10)**.
- The **9** is in the **hundredths** place, representing **nine-hundredths (0.09 or 9/100)**.
- The **6** is in the **thousandths** place, representing **six-thousandths (0.006 or 6/1000)**.

When you read or write large numbers, it's essential to recognize the position of each digit and understand the place values to express the number in words. For example, **4,312.796** is read as "**four thousand, three hundred twelve and seven hundred ninety-six thousandths.**"

Now let's consider how to convert number names into digits. This can sometimes seem tricky, but with practice, it's straightforward. The key is breaking down the number name into its components and assigning each part to its appropriate place value.

If you're asked to write the number two hundred forty-three thousand, fifty-eight in digits, it would look like this:

- **Two hundred forty-three thousand= 243,000**
- **Fifty-eight= 58**

Therefore, the full number is: **243,058**.

Remember, this is a section where you should be picking up easy marks. Make sure to not make silly mistakes. Here are some common mistakes students make:

1. **Misunderstanding Place Value**: One common mistake when reading number names is misinterpreting the place value of digits. For example, **"ten thousand, five hundred"** is written as **10,500**, not **105,000**. Pay close attention to the word "thousand" to ensure you're placing digits correctly.
2. **Confusing Fractions**: When writing fractional numbers, the terms **tenths, hundredths,** and **thousandths** should be clearly understood. A number like **0.45** is read as **"forty-five hundredths,"** not **"four and fifty."**
3. **Missing Hyphens in Compound Numbers**: When writing numbers like twenty-one, thirty-five, or ninety-nine, remember that these compound numbers require hyphens. **Twenty-one**, not **twenty one**.

Number Name Questions and Answers

Understanding the relationship between numerals and their written word counterparts is a fundamental skill in mathematics. Let's explore some examples to solidify this concept:

Example 1: Numerals to Words

- **Question:** Write, in words, the number "3,427".
- **Solution:**

1. **Break it down:**

    o 3 is in the thousands place: three thousand
    o 4 is in the hundreds place: three thousand four hundred
    o 2 is in the tens place: three thousand four hundred twenty
    o 7 is in the ones place: three thousand four hundred twenty-seven

- **Answer:** Three thousand four hundred twenty-seven

Example 2: Words to Numerals

- **Question:** Write, in numerals, "six thousand eighty-two."
- **Solution:**

    1. **Identify place values:**

        - Six thousand: 6,000
        - Eighty: 80
        - Two: 2

    2. **Combine:** 6,000 + 80 + 2 = 6,082

- **Answer:** 6,082

Here are some practice problems for you to try:

1. Write, in numerals: "nine thousand five hundred thirteen"
2. Write, in words: 4,038
3. Write, in numerals: "seven hundred six"
4. Write, in words: 1,200

Answers:

1. 9,513
2. Four thousand thirty-eight
3. 706
4. One thousand two hundred

Fraction Problems

Fractions often appear in HSPT math questions. However, fractions are nothing to fear once you break them down and understand their core concepts.

A fraction represents a part of a whole. Imagine this scenario: You have a pizza cut into 8 equal slices, and you've eaten 3 of them. The fraction **3/8** describes what part of the pizza you've consumed. In this case, the **3** represents the slices you ate, and the **8** represents the total number of slices, giving you a clear picture of the portion you've enjoyed.

To make sure you're fully prepared for any fraction-related question on the HSPT, it's essential to understand the three main types of fractions:

1. **Proper Fractions**: These are fractions where the top number (the numerator) is less than the bottom number (the denominator). Examples include **1/2, 3/4,** and **9/10**. The value of a proper fraction is always less than 1.
2. **Improper Fractions**: In these fractions, the numerator is greater than or equal to the denominator. Examples are **5/4, 9/7,** and **13/8**. The value of an improper fraction is 1 or more.
3. **Mixed Numbers**: A mixed number combines a whole number with a fraction. For example, **2 3/4** means you have 2 whole parts and 3 out of 4 equal parts. Mixed numbers represent values greater than 1 and are often easier to visualize, especially when dealing with real-world situations.

Changing Improper Fractions to Mixed Numbers

Sometimes, it's easier to work with mixed numbers instead of improper fractions, especially when adding or subtracting. Let's look at how to convert an improper fraction, like 13/2, into a mixed number:

1. Divide the numerator (13) by the denominator (2): **13 ÷ 2= 6** with a remainder of **1**.
2. The whole number part of the mixed number is **6**.
3. The remainder, **1**, becomes the numerator of the fraction, with the original denominator (**2**) staying the same.

Thus, **13/2** becomes **6½**.

Changing Mixed Numbers to Improper Fractions

On the other hand, when multiplying or dividing fractions, it's often more convenient to work with improper fractions. Here's how you can convert a mixed number like **2 3/4** into an improper fraction:

1. Multiply the whole number (**2**) by the denominator (**4**): **2 × 4= 8**.
2. Add the result (**8**) to the numerator (**3**): **8 + 3= 11**.
3. The improper fraction is **11/4**.

Reducing Fractions

One of the most important skills when working with fractions is reducing them to their lowest terms. Reducing a fraction doesn't change its value; it just simplifies it, making calculations easier. Here's how you can reduce the fraction 8/12:

1. Find a number that divides evenly into both the numerator and denominator. In this case, **4** works because both **8 and 12** are divisible by **4**.
2. Divide both the numerator and denominator by **4**:

    o 8 ÷ 4= 2
    o 12 ÷ 4= 3

Thus, **8/12** reduces to **2/3**.

If both the numerator and denominator end in zeros, you can quickly reduce the fraction by crossing out the same number of zeroes from both the top and bottom. If you have **300/600**, you can cross out two zeros from both numbers to get **3/6**, which simplifies to **1/2**.

Here are some sample questions for you:

1. Reduce the fraction 4/8 to its lowest terms.

Explanation:

To reduce a fraction to its lowest terms, we need to find the **greatest common factor (GCF)** of the numerator and denominator and then divide both by the GCF.

In this case, the GCF of 4 and 8 is 4.

Dividing both the numerator and denominator by 4, we get:

4 ÷ 4 / 8 ÷ 4= 1/2

Answer: 1/2

2. Simplify the fraction 15/25.

Explanation: The GCF of 15 and 25 is 5.

Dividing both by 5, we get:

15 ÷ 5 / 25 ÷ 5= 3/5

Answer: 3/5

3. Reduce the fraction 24/36 to its simplest form.

Explanation: The GCF of 24 and 36 is 12.

Dividing both by 12, we get:

24 ÷ 12 / 36 ÷ 12= 2/3

Answer: 2/3

4. Simplify the fraction 10/15.

Explanation: The GCF of 10 and 15 is 5.

Dividing both by 5, we get:

10 ÷ 5 / 15 ÷ 5= 2/3

Answer: 2/3

5. Reduce the fraction 18/27 to its lowest terms.

Explanation: The GCF of 18 and 27 is 9.

Dividing both by 9, we get:

18 ÷ 9 / 27 ÷ 9= 2/3

Answer: 2/3

Raising Fractions to Higher Terms

Raising a fraction to higher terms is the reverse of reducing a fraction. It means multiplying both the numerator and denominator by the same number to create an equivalent fraction with larger numbers. This skill is particularly useful when you need to manipulate fractions to make them easier to add or subtract.

Here's an example: Let's raise the fraction **2/3** to 24ths.

1. Start by dividing the denominator of the original fraction (3) into the new denominator (24):

   24 ÷ 3= 8

2. Multiply both the numerator and denominator by 8 to scale the fraction up:

   (2 × 8) / (3 × 8) = 16/24

3. Check your work by reducing **16/24** back to its original form:

   16/24 → 2/3 (success!)

   Thus, **2/3** raised to 24ths is **16/24**.

Adding Fractions

Adding Fractions with the Same Denominator

When adding fractions with the same denominator, the process is straightforward—just add the numerators and keep the denominator unchanged. This makes the task simple and efficient.

For example:

2/9 + 4/9 = (2 + 4)/9 = 6/9

You can simplify this fraction further by reducing it:

6/9 = 2/3

Here's another example with mixed numbers:

3 5/8 + 7 1/8

1. First, add the whole numbers:

   3 + 7 = 10

2. Then, add the fractions:

    5/8 + 1/8= 6/8 (which simplifies to **3/4**)

3. The result is:

    10 + 3/4= 10 3/4

Adding mixed numbers becomes just as easy once you follow these steps.

Adding Fractions with Different Denominators

When you're adding fractions that don't have the same denominator, you need to find the **least common denominator (LCD)** before you can proceed. This involves raising the fractions to equivalent fractions with the same denominator.

Here's how you can approach it:

1. **Find the LCD**:

    For **2/3 + 4/5**, the denominators are **3** and **5**. The LCD is the smallest number that both 3 and 5 divide into evenly. The **LCD** of 3 and 5 is **15**.

2. **Raise both fractions to 15ths**:

    Multiply **2/3** by **5/5** and **4/5** by **3/3** to get:

    2/3= 10/15 and **4/5= 12/15**

3. **Add the fractions**:

    Now that both fractions have the same denominator, you can simply add the numerators:

    10/15 + 12/15= 22/15

4. **Convert to a mixed number:**

   22/15 is an improper fraction, so convert it to a mixed number:

   22 ÷ 15 = 1 remainder 7, so the mixed number is **1 7/15**.

Finding the Least Common Denominator (LCD)

When adding fractions with different denominators, finding the LCD is a crucial step. Here's a deeper dive into finding the LCD:

- **Step 1**: Look at the largest denominator and check if all the smaller denominators divide evenly into it. If they do, that's your LCD.
- **Step 2**: If the largest denominator doesn't work, look at the multiplication table of the largest denominator until you find a number that all other denominators divide into evenly.
- **Step 3**: If that doesn't work, you can always multiply all the denominators together to find a common denominator. While this works, it may not always give the least common denominator.

Let's take another example: **2/3 + 4/5**

1. The **LCD** of 3 and 5 is **15** (as we saw earlier).
2. Raise the fractions to **15ths**:

   o **2/3 becomes 10/15**
   o **4/5 becomes 12/15**

3. Now add the fractions:

   10/15 + 12/15 = 22/15

And there you have it—adding fractions with different denominators made easy!

Subtracting Fractions

Subtracting Fractions with the Same Denominator

When the fractions have the same denominator, subtracting them is a straightforward process. The rule is simple: subtract the numerators and keep the denominator the same. This makes subtracting fractions relatively easy.

Example 1:

4/9 - 3/9

- Subtract the numerators:
  4 - 3 = 1

- Keep the denominator the same:
  1/9

Thus, **4/9 - 3/9 = 1/9**.

Subtracting Fractions with Different Denominators

When the fractions you want to subtract have different denominators, the process becomes slightly more complex. First, you need to find the **Least Common Denominator (LCD)**, just like when adding fractions with different denominators. Once you've found the LCD, raise both fractions to equivalent fractions with that common denominator, and then perform the subtraction.

Example 2:
5/6 - 3/4

1. **Find the LCD**: The least common denominator between 6 and 4 is **12**.
2. **Raise each fraction to 12ths**:
    - **5/6** becomes **10/12** (because 5 × 2 = 10, and 6 × 2 = 12)
    - **3/4** becomes **9/12** (because 3 × 3 = 9, and 4 × 3 = 12)

3. **Subtract the fractions**:
   10/12 - 9/12 = 1/12

Thus, **5/6 - 3/4 = 1/12**.

Subtracting Mixed Numbers

When subtracting **mixed numbers** (numbers with a whole number and a fraction), the process is similar to adding mixed numbers. You subtract the fractions first, and then subtract the whole numbers. However, sometimes you may need to **borrow** when the fraction in the minuend (the number you're subtracting from) is smaller than the fraction in the subtrahend (the number you're subtracting).

Example 3:
4 3/5 - 1 2/5

1. **Subtract the fractions**:
   3/5 - 2/5 = 1/5
2. **Subtract the whole numbers**:
   4 - 1 = 3

Thus, **4 3/5 - 1 = 3 1/5**

Borrowing When Subtracting Mixed Numbers

In some cases, you may need to borrow when subtracting mixed numbers, especially when the fraction in the subtrahend is larger than the fraction in the minuend.

Example 4:
7 3/5 - 2 4/5

1. You can't subtract **4/5** from **3/5** because **4/5** is greater than **3/5**. So, **borrow** 1 from the whole number **7**, turning it into **6**, and add **5/5** to **3/5**. Now, you have:
   7 3/5 = 6 8/5.

2. Now subtract the fractions:
   $8/5 - 4/5 = 4/5$
3. Subtract the whole numbers:
   6 - 2 = 4

Thus, **7 3/5 - 2 4/5 = 4 4/5**

Solving Real-Life Problems with Fractions

Understanding how to subtract fractions is not only vital for mathematical exercises but also for real-life scenarios where calculations involve measurements, distances, and quantities.

Example:

Alan's Total Travel Distance

Alan drove a total of several distances, which involved both whole numbers and fractions. He drove:

- 3 ½ miles to school
- 4 ¾ miles to football practice
- 2 miles to meet friends
- 3 ⅔ miles back to school
- Finally, 3 ½ miles home.

To calculate Alan's total travel distance, we will add the distances:

1. 3 ½ + 4 ¾ + 2 + 3 ⅔ + 3½
   This requires adding the whole numbers and the fractions separately.

2. **Add the whole numbers**:
   3 + 4 + 2 + 3 + 3 = 15
3. **Add the fractions**:
   Convert all the fractions to have the same denominator and add them:

   o   1/2 + 3/4 + 2/3 + 1/2

1. **Total travel distance= 16 ¼ miles** (after performing the calculations with proper LCDs and addition).

Fraction Practice Problems

Now that you've grasped the steps involved in subtracting fractions and solving real-world fraction problems, it's time to put your knowledge to work with some practice problems.

- **Problem 1**: 4 ⅖ - 3
- **Problem 2**: 7 ⅛ - 4 ⅔
- **Problem 3**: 4 ⅓ - 2 ¾
- **Problem 4**: Alan drove 3 ½ miles, then 4 ¾ miles. How far did he drive in total?

Multiplying Fractions: The Simplicity of Scaling

Multiplying fractions is refreshingly straightforward. All you need to do is multiply the numerators (top numbers) and then the denominators (bottom numbers). The result is a new fraction that represents the product.

Example:

$$\frac{2}{3} \times \frac{5}{7} = \frac{2 \times 5}{3 \times 7} = \frac{10}{21}$$

Quick Tip: Cancel before you multiply. To simplify calculations, cancel common factors between numerators and denominators before multiplying. This process reduces the fraction early, saving time and effort.

Example with Cancellation:

$$\frac{6}{9} \times \frac{20}{15}$$

1. Simplify: 6÷3= 2, 9 ÷ 3= 3, 20 ÷5= 4, 15÷5= 3.
2. Multiply the reduced fractions:

$$\frac{2}{3} \times \frac{4}{3} = \frac{8}{9}$$

This approach works seamlessly with whole numbers and mixed fractions too. Just convert them into improper fractions first.

Example:

Multiply 4⅔× 5×½:

1. Convert: 4⅔ – ¹⁴⁄₃=, 5½ =¹¹⁄₂.
2. Multiply:

$$\frac{14}{3} \times \frac{11}{2} = \frac{154}{6} = 25\frac{2}{3}$$

Dividing Fractions

Division of fractions may sound tricky, but it's as simple as flipping the script—literally. To divide one fraction by another, invert (flip) the second fraction and change the division sign to multiplication. Then multiply as usual.

Example:

$$\frac{1}{2} \div \frac{3}{5}$$

1. Flip: The second fraction becomes 5/3
2. Multiply:

$$\frac{1}{2} \times \frac{5}{3} = \frac{5}{6}$$

Dividing with Whole Numbers and Mixed Fractions

When dividing by a whole number, convert it into a fraction by placing it over 1. For mixed fractions, convert to improper fractions first.

Example:
Divide 3¾÷2:

1. Convert: 3¾=15/4, and 2 =2/1.
2. Flip and Multiply:

$$\frac{15}{4} \div \frac{2}{1} = \frac{15}{4} \times \frac{1}{2} = \frac{15}{8} = 1\frac{7}{8}$$

Real-World Fraction Scenarios

These practical examples showcase the power of multiplying and dividing fractions:

1. **Travel Distances:**

   Dr. Stone drove ⅔ of 15 miles before an emergency call. How far did he drive?

$$\frac{2}{3} \times 15 = \frac{30}{3} = 10 \text{ miles.}$$

2. **Work Hours:**

   Henry spent ¾ of his 40-hour work week in training. How many hours was that?

   $$\frac{3}{4} \times 40 = 30 \text{ hours.}$$

3. **Pay Calculation:**

   Technician Chin works 11 hours, with overtime pay at 1½ times the regular rate of $14/hour for hours beyond 8. Her total earnings:

   $$8 \times 14 + 3 \times 14 \times \frac{3}{2} = 112 + 63 = 175 \text{ dollars.}$$

4. **Sharing Candy:**

   Dr. McCarthy's four assistants divided 6½ pounds of candy evenly. Each received:

   $$\frac{13}{2} \div 4 = \frac{13}{8} = 1\frac{5}{8} \text{ pounds.}$$

Practice Problems

Try these to test your understanding.

1. ⅕ × ⅔
2. ¾ ÷ ⅝
3. Multiply 2½ × 6.
4. Divide 33⅘ ÷ 21⅗.

Answers:

1. Multiply the numerators and the denominators:

$$\frac{1 \times 2}{5 \times 3} = \frac{2}{15}$$

Answer: 2/15

2. Flip the second fraction and multiply:

$$\frac{3 \times 2}{1 \times 5} = \frac{6}{5}$$

Cancel the 4 and the 8: 8÷4= 2.

Multiply:

$$\frac{6}{5} = 1\frac{1}{5}$$

Convert to a mixed number:

Answer: 1⅕

3. Multiply 2½ ×6:

Convert 2½ to an improper fraction:

$$2\frac{1}{2} = \frac{5}{2}$$

Rewrite 6 as a fraction:

$$6 = \frac{6}{1}$$

Multiply the fractions:

$$\frac{5}{2} \times \frac{6}{1} = \frac{30}{2} = 15$$

Answer: 15

4. Divide $33\frac{4}{5} \div 21\frac{3}{5}$.:

Convert both mixed numbers to improper fractions:

$$33\frac{4}{5} = \frac{169}{5}, \quad 21\frac{3}{5} = \frac{108}{5}$$

Divide by flipping the second fraction and multiplying:

$$\frac{169}{5} \div \frac{108}{5} = \frac{169}{5} \times \frac{5}{108}$$

Cancel the 5s:

$$\frac{169 \times 1}{1 \times 108} = \frac{169}{108}$$

Simplify (if needed): 169/108 is already in simplest form.

Convert to a mixed number:

$$\frac{169}{108} = 1\frac{61}{108}$$

Answer: $1\frac{61}{108}$

Comparing Fractions

Fractions often appear in scenarios that demand a keen eye for comparison, whether it's dividing a pizza among friends or analyzing mathematical problems.

When Denominators Are the Same

Fractions with identical denominators are the easiest to compare. The denominator tells us how many equal parts the whole is divided. When this number is the same for two fractions, the size of the fraction depends entirely on the numerator.

Example:

Which is larger: $2/5$ or $3/5$?

Imagine a pie sliced into five equal pieces. If you take two pieces, you have $2/5$, but taking three pieces gives $3/5$. Naturally, $3/5$ is larger because you have more of the pie.

Key Insight:

When denominators are equal, just compare the numerators. The fraction with the larger numerator is the larger fraction.

When Numerators Are the Same

When two fractions share the same numerator, the comparison shifts to their denominators. The denominator tells us how many parts the whole is divided into, so a larger denominator means each part is smaller.

Example:

Which is smaller: $3/5$ or $3/7$?

Imagine two pies, one divided into 5 pieces and the other into 7. If you take three pieces from each pie, the pieces from the pie divided into 7 parts (3/7) will be smaller. Therefore, 3/7 is less than 3/5.

Key Insight:

When numerators are equal, the fraction with the larger denominator is the smaller fraction.

When Both Numerators and Denominators Differ

When fractions have different numerators and denominators, the comparison requires aligning them to a common denominator. This ensures a fair comparison by equalizing the size of the parts being considered.

Steps to Compare Fractions with Different Denominators:

1. **Find a Common Denominator:** Identify the least common multiple (LCM) of the denominators.
2. **Adjust the Fractions:** Rewrite each fraction with the common denominator.
3. **Compare the New Numerators:** The fraction with the larger numerator is larger.

Example:

Compare 2/3 and 3/4.

1. The LCM of 3 and 4 is 12.
2. Rewrite the fractions:

$$\frac{2}{3} = \frac{8}{12}, \quad \frac{3}{4} = \frac{9}{12}$$

3. Compare 8/12 and 9/12:

    Since 9 is greater than 8, 3/4 is larger than 2/3.

Real-World Applications

Comparing fractions isn't limited to theoretical exercises—it has real-life relevance. Whether you're dividing resources, analyzing data, or making informed decisions, understanding fractional relationships equips you to approach problems logically and efficiently.

For instance, consider dividing a 12-slice pizza among two groups: one receiving 7/12 and the other 5/12. A quick comparison shows that the first group gets more slices, making 7/12 the larger share.

Practice Problems

1. Which is larger: 4/9 or 5/9?
2. Which is smaller: 2/7 or 2/5?
3. Compare 3/8 and 5/12.

Use these exercises to solidify your skills. Remember, mastering fractions is a step toward mathematical confidence and practical problem-solving

Decimals

Decimals offer practical, everyday application—think of the times you've calculated the price of groceries or read the weight of an object on a scale. This section dives into the fundamentals of decimals, empowering you with the confidence to tackle them in any context.

A decimal is essentially a special form of a fraction. Instead of representing parts of a whole with a numerator and denominator, decimals use a dot—the decimal point—to separate whole numbers from fractional parts.

When you see $10.35, the number represents 10 dollars and 35 cents. The decimal point acts as the boundary, with whole dollars on the left and fractional cents on the right.

Decimal Place Values:

Each digit to the right of the decimal point has a specific value:

- 0.1: **One-tenth** or ¹⁄₁₀
- 0.01: **One-hundredth** or ¹⁄₁₀₀
- 0.001: **One-thousandth** or ¹⁄₁₀₀₀
- 0.0001: **One ten-thousandth** or ¹⁄₁₀₀₀₀

Adding zeros to the right of a decimal doesn't change its value. For example:

$$6.17 = 6.170 = 6.1700$$

This characteristic ensures that decimals maintain their precision without altering their numerical meaning.

Types of Decimals

1. **Pure Decimals:** Numbers with only digits to the right of the decimal point (e.g., 0.53).
2. **Mixed Decimals:** Numbers with both whole numbers and decimal parts (e.g., 10.35).
3. **Whole Numbers as Decimals:** Every whole number can be expressed as a decimal (e.g., 15 is the same as 15.0, 15.00, and so on).

Understanding these distinctions is crucial when working with decimals in various mathematical contexts.

Converting Fractions to Decimals

Changing a fraction to a decimal involves simple division: divide the numerator (top number) by the denominator (bottom number).

Example: Convert ¾ to a decimal:

1. Add a decimal point and two zeroes to the numerator: 3.00.
2. Divide the denominator into the numerator: 4 into 3.00= 0.75.
3. The result, 0.75 is the decimal equivalent of ¾

Some fractions result in repeating decimals, such as ⅔ :

2÷3= 0.666... (repeating)

This can be represented as 0.$\underline{6}$ approximated as 0.67 depending on the level of precision needed.

Converting Decimals to Fractions

To convert a decimal into a fraction:

1. Write the digits of the decimal as the numerator.
2. Determine the place value of the last decimal digit and use it as the denominator.
3. Simplify the fraction if possible.

Example: Convert 0.018 to a fraction:

1. Write 18 as the numerator.
2. Since 0.018 ends in the thousandths place, the denominator is 1,000:

$$18/1000$$

3. Simplify by dividing both numerator and denominator by their greatest common factor:

$$18/1000 = 9/500$$

Practice Problems

1. Convert 0.005 into a fraction.
2. Convert 3.48 into a fraction.
3. Convert 123.456 into a fraction.

Comparing Decimals

When comparing decimals, it's helpful to ensure that all decimals have the same number of digits after the decimal point. By doing so, you eliminate any confusion and make the comparison more straightforward.

Example: Compare 0.08 and 0.1

1. Add a zero to 0.1, turning it into 0.10
2. Compare as whole numbers: 10>8.
3. Conclusion: 0.1 is larger than 0.08

This simple strategy can be applied to decimals with multiple digits, ensuring clarity and accuracy.

Adding and Subtracting Decimals

Adding and subtracting decimals is as easy as aligning the decimal points and working with the numbers as if they were whole numbers. If the decimals have varying lengths, add zeros to the shorter numbers to ensure proper alignment.

Addition Example: 1.23+57+0.038

1. Line up the numbers:

$$\begin{array}{r} 1.230 \\ 57.000 \\ +0.038 \end{array}$$

2. Add: 58.268

Subtraction Example: 1.23-0.0381.23 - 0.0381.23-0.038

1. Line up the numbers:

$$1.230$$
$$-0.038$$

2. Subtract: 1.192

Proper alignment of decimal points ensures precision in every calculation.

Real-Life Problem Applications: Addition and Subtraction

1. **Total Miles Driven:**

   James Peterson drove the following distances:

   - 3.7 miles to the sports club
   - 2.75 miles to the juice bar
   - 2 miles back home

Total miles driven:

$$3.7+2.75+2= 8.45 \text{ miles.}$$

Correct answer: **8.45**

2. **Emergency Room Visits:**

   The average weekly visits decreased from 486.4 to 402.5

   Decrease:

$$486.4-402.5= 83.9 \text{ visits.}$$

Correct answer: **83.9**

Multiplying Decimals

Multiplying decimals involves a two-step process:

1. Ignore the decimal points and multiply as if working with whole numbers.
2. Count the total number of decimal places in the factors, and apply that many decimal places to the result.

Example 1: 215.7×2.4

1. Multiply 2157×24=51,768
2. Count the decimal places: 1+1= 2
3. Place the decimal point: 517.68

Example 2: 0.03×0.006

1. Multiply 3×6=18
2. Total decimal places: 2+3= 5.
3. Add zeroes and place the decimal point: 0.00018.

Real-Life Problem Applications: Multiplication

1. **Earnings Calculation:** Joe earns $14.50 per hour and worked 37.5 hours.

    14.50×37.5= 543.75

    Answer: **$543.75**

2. **Cost of Nuts:** Nuts cost $3.50 per pound. For 4.25 pounds:

    3.50×4.25=14.88

    Answer: **$14.88**

Practice Problems

Try solving these problems to reinforce your understanding:

1. 0.905+0.02+3.075
2. 3.48−2.573
3. 0.05×0.6
4. 38.1×0.0184

Dividing Decimals

Dividing decimals might seem challenging at first glance, but with the right techniques and mindset, it becomes an empowering tool for solving everyday problems

Dividing Decimals by Whole Numbers

When dividing a decimal by a whole number, the process is straightforward. The key is to maintain the position of the decimal point in the answer.

Example: Divide 0.256 by 8.

1. Set up the division: 8 / 0.256.
2. Move the decimal point in the dividend (0.256) straight up into the answer line.

$$\begin{array}{r} .032 \\ 8{\overline{\smash{\big)}\,.256}} \\ \underline{0} \\ 25 \\ \underline{24} \\ 16 \\ \underline{16} \\ 0 \end{array}$$

3. Divide as you would with whole numbers: 8/2.56→0.032

The quotient is **0.032**.

Dividing Decimals by Decimals

When dividing by a decimal, there's an essential extra step: convert the divisor into a whole number by moving the decimal point to the right. Apply the same shift to the dividend.

Example: Divide 1.218 by 0.06

1. Move the decimal in 0.06 two places to the right, turning it into 6. Do the same to 1.218, converting it into 121.8

$$.06.\overline{)1.21\overset{.}{8}}$$

$$\begin{array}{r} 20.3 \\ 6\overline{)121.8} \\ \underline{12} \\ 01 \\ \underline{00} \\ 18 \\ \underline{18} \\ 0 \end{array}$$

2. Perform the division: 6/121.8=20.3.

The quotient is **20.3**.

Handling Special Cases in Division

Sometimes, division doesn't result in a clean answer. Here's how to handle specific scenarios:

- **Not enough digits:** Add zeros to the dividend to continue dividing.

- **Uneven results:** Continue dividing to reach the desired level of precision.
- **Whole number divided by a decimal:** Shift the decimal point as needed and add zeros to the dividend.

These strategies ensure accuracy, even in the most complex problems.

Real-Life Problem Applications: Division

1. **Motorcycle Speed Calculation:**

   James Worthington drove 92.4 miles in 2.1 hours. To find his average speed:

   $$92.4 / 2.1 = 44. \text{ Miles per hour}$$

   Answer: **44.**

2. **Mary Sanders' Walking Average:**

   Mary walked 18.6 miles over 4 days. To find her daily average:

   $$18.6 / 4 = 4.65$$

   Answer: **4.65.**

Practice Problems

Here are a few division problems to test your skills:

1. 9.8÷7
2. 0.0512÷0.0004
3. 28.6÷0.05
4. 196÷0.14

Percents

Percents offer a unique way to represent portions of a whole. Whether you're calculating discounts, interpreting interest rates, or analyzing data, understanding percents unlocks countless practical applications.

A percent represents a fraction where the denominator is always 100. The term "percent" originates from the Latin word *centum*, meaning 100, similar to how a century equals 100 years or a dollar is divided into 100 cents.

For instance, 17% means $17/100$, which is equivalent to 0.17 in decimal form or 17 parts out of 100.

You encounter percents in many aspects of life:

- **Sales Tax:** A percentage of the purchase price.
- **Discounts:** Percent reductions during sales.
- **Interest Rates:** Expressed as a percentage for loans and savings.

Changing Decimals to Percents (and Vice Versa)

From Decimal to Percent:

- Move the decimal point **two places to the right**.
- Add a percent sign (%) at the end.

Examples:

- 0.45= 45%
- 0.008= 0.8%
- 0.162=16.2%

From Percent to Decimal:

- Remove the percent sign (%).
- Move the decimal point **two places to the left**.

Examples:

- 12%= 0.12
- 87.5%= 0.875
- 250%= 2.5

Changing Fractions to Percents (and Vice Versa)

From Fraction to Percent:

There are two techniques for converting a fraction to a percent:

Technique 1: Multiply the Fraction by 100%.

$$¼ \times 100\% = 25\%$$

Technique 2: Divide the Numerator by the Denominator, then Convert to Percent.

Move the decimal two places right:

$$¼ = 0.25 = 25\%$$

From Percent to Fraction:

1. Remove the percent sign (%).
2. Write the number as a fraction over 100100100.
3. Simplify if possible.

Examples:

- 4%= 4/100 = 1/25

- 87.5% = $^{87.5}/_{100}$ = $^{875}/_{1000}$ = ⅞
- 125% = $^{125}/_{100}$ = 5/4

Practice and Real-Life Applications

- Convert 0.45, 0.008, and 0.162 to percentages.
- Convert 12%, 87.5%, and 250 % to decimals.
- Convert ⅛, ⅓ and ⅖ to percents.
- Convert 95%, 37.5%, and 125% to fractions.

The Three Types of Percent Problems

1. Find a Percent of a Whole

    Example: What is 30% of 40?

In this case, the percent (30%) and the whole (40) are given, and the task is to determine the part.

2. Find What Percent One Number is of Another

    Example: 12 is what percent of 40?

Here, the part (12) and the whole (40) are provided, and you need to find the percent.

3. Find the Whole When the Percent of It is Given

    Example: 12 is 30% of what number?

The percent (30%) and the part (12) are given, and you must calculate the whole.

For all these problems, a simple formula comes to the rescue:

$$\frac{\text{part}}{\text{whole}} = \frac{\%}{100}$$

Using cross-multiplication, we can solve for any missing variable, whether it's the part, whole, or percent.

Step-by-Step Solutions with Examples

1. Find a Percent of a Whole

   Example: What is 30% of 40?

   Here, 30 is the percent, and 40 is the whole. Plug into the formula:

   $$is/40 = 30/100$$

   Cross-multiply and solve:

   $$is \times 100 = 40 \times 30$$
   $$is \times 100 = 1,200$$
   $$is = 12$$

   Answer: 30% of 40 is 12.

2. Find What Percent One Number is of Another

   Example: 12 is what percent of 40?

   Here, 12 is the part, and 40 is the whole. Use the formula:

   $$12/40 = \%/100$$

   $$12/\text{whole} = 30/100$$

   Cross-multiply and solve:

$$12 \times 100 = 40 \times \%$$

$$1,200 = 40 \times \%$$

$$\% = 30$$

Answer: 12 is 30% of 40.

3. Find the Whole When the Percent of It is Given

    Example: 12 is 30% of what number?

    Here, 12 is the part, and 30 is the percent. Use the formula:

    $$12/\text{whole} = 30/100$$

Cross-multiply and solve:

$$12 \times 100 = \text{whole} \times 30$$

$$1,200 = \text{whole} \times 30$$

$$\text{whole} = 40$$

Answer: 12 is 30% of 40.

Percent Change: Increase or Decrease

1. **Calculating Percent Decrease:** A merchant reduces the price of $20 hats to $15. By what percent is the price decreased?

    The decrease is 20 −15= 5

    Use the original price (20) as the whole:

    $$5/20 = \%/100$$

    Cross-multiply:

$$5 \times 100 = 20 \times \%$$

$$500 = 20 \times \%$$

$$\% = 25$$

Answer: The price has decreased by **25%**.

2. **Calculating Percent Increase** If the price increases from $15 to $20, what is the percent increase?

The increase is 20 −15= 5

Use the new base price (15) as the whole:

$$5/15 = \%/100$$

Cross-multiply:

$$5 \times 100 = 15 \times \%$$

$$500 = 15 \times \%$$

$$\% \approx 33.33$$

Answer: The price is increased by **33.33%**

Conversion Table for Efficiency

Here's a handy table to memorize key conversions for quick calculations:

Decimal	Percent	Fraction
0.25	25%	¼
0.50	50%	½

0.75	75%	¾
0.333	33.33%	⅓
0.666	66.67%	⅔

Averages

An average represents the "center" of a group of numbers. It helps answer questions like: *What is typical? What can I expect?* For example:

- Your **bowling average** tells how well you perform over multiple games.
- The **class average score** helps determine the general performance of students in a test.
- The **average speed** on a journey tells you how fast you were moving overall.

In short, averages give meaning to a collection of numbers, making comparisons and decisions easier.

How to Calculate an Average

The formula for finding an average is straightforward:

Average= Sum of All Values \ Number of Values

1. Add all the numbers in the set together to get the total sum.
2. Divide this sum by the number of values in the set.
3. The result is the average.

Example 1: Simple Average Calculation

Question: What is the average of 6, 10, and 20?

1. Add the numbers: 6+10+20= 36.
2. Divide by the total count: 36/ 3= 12

Answer: The average is **12**.

Weighted Averages: A Practical Twist

Sometimes, not all numbers carry the same weight or importance in the calculation. In such cases, a **weighted average** is used.

Example:

In a lifeguard course, there are 10 females with an average score of 85 and 20 males with an average score of 95. What is the overall class average?

1. Multiply each group's average by the number of people in the group:

    o Females: 85×10= 850
    o Males: 95×20=1,900
    o Add the results: 850+1,900= 2,750

2. Divide by the total number of students: 2,750/ 30 = 91.67.

    Answer: The class average is approximately **91.67**.

Tip: Weighted averages ensure that larger groups have a proportional impact on the final result.

Calculating Averages in Special Scenarios

1. **Averages Across Different Speeds**

    When calculating average speed over varying distances or time, use this formula:

    $$\text{Average Speed} = \frac{\text{Total Distance}}{\text{Total Time}}$$

    Example: Conroy drives at 30 mph for 2 hours in town and 60 mph for 2 hours on the highway.

- o Calculate the total distance: (30×2)+(60×2)=60+120=180 miles
- o Calculate the total time: 2+2= 4 hours.
- o Divide: 180/ 4 = 45.

Answer: The average speed is **45 mph**.

2. **Combining Multiple Averages**

   Avoid the common trap of directly averaging given averages. Always account for the weight of each group (e.g., the number of people, items, or occurrences)

Practice Problems

1. Bob's bowling scores over five games were 180, 182, 184, 186, and 188. What was his average score?

   o **Hint:** Add the scores and divide by 5.

2. Conroy drove 30 miles an hour for 2 hours in town and 60 miles an hour for 2 hours on the highway. What was his average speed?

   o **Hint:** Total the distance and divide by the total time.

3. In a lifeguard class, 10 females scored an average of 85, and 20 males scored an average of 95. What was the overall class average?

   o **Hint:** Use weighted averages.

Length, Weight, and Time Units:

Units of length, weight, and time are the building blocks of daily measurement tasks, appearing in everything from planning schedules to crafting projects. Let's explore how to tackle these concepts with confidence and clarity for your HSPT exam.

Converting Between Units

Conversions between measurement units follow a simple principle:

- To convert from a smaller unit to a larger unit: Divide by the conversion factor.
- To convert from a larger unit to a smaller unit: Multiply by the conversion factor

Length Conversions

- Example 1: Convert 36 inches to feet.
  Since 1 foot=12 inches, divide: 36/12= 3 feet

- Example 2: Convert 4 feet to inches.
  Multiply: 4×12=48 inches

Weight Conversions

- **Example 1:** Convert 32 ounces to pounds.
  Since 1 pound=16 ounces
  Divide:
  32/16= 2 pounds

- **Example 2:** Convert 2 pounds to ounces.
  Multiply:
  2×16= 32 ounces

Time Conversions

- **Example 1:** Convert 180 minutes to hours.
  Since 1 hour= 60 minutes
  Divide:
  180/60= 3 hours

- **Example 2:** Convert 4 hours to minutes.

Multiply:
4×60= 240 minutes.

Practice Questions for Conversion

1. **Convert 2 feet to inches:**
   - 2×12= ?

2. **Convert 3 pounds to ounces:**
   - 3×16= ?

3. **Convert 2 hours to minutes:**
   - 2×60= ?

4. **Convert 120 minutes to hours:**
   - 120/60= ?

Adding and Subtracting Units

When adding or subtracting measurements, always separate units (feet, inches, hours, minutes, etc.) and convert if necessary to maintain consistency.

Adding Length Units

Example: Add the following lengths:

- 6 feet 9 inches
- 5 feet 7 inches
- 3 feet 5 inches

1. Add feet: 6+5+3=14 feet.
2. Add inches: 9+7+5= 21 inches.
3. Convert extra inches to feet:
   o   21 inches= 1 foot 9 inches.
4. Total: 14 feet +1 foot 9 inches= 15 feet 9 inches.

Subtracting Length Units

Example: Subtract 3 feet 8 inches from 9 feet 3 inches.

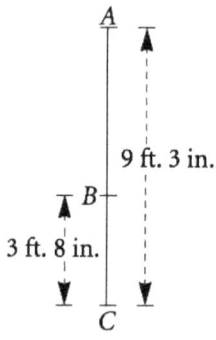

1. Since 8 inches > 3 inches, borrow 1 foot (12 inches) from the feet column:

   o   9 feet 3 inches= 8 feet 15 inches.

2. Subtract:

   o   Inches: 15 – 8= 7 inches.
   o   Feet: 8 – 3= 5 feet

Answer: 5 feet 7 inches.

Here are some tips to make sure you don't miss out on these conversions

1. Always double-check conversions before performing any addition or subtraction.
2. When converting smaller units (like inches) into larger ones (like feet), don't forget to carry over extra values.

Algebra

Algebra is the language of problem-solving and critical thinking. The **math test** will assess various algebraic skills, including:

- Solving equations: Unraveling the value of unknown variables.
- Understanding positive and negative numbers: Working seamlessly with numbers on both sides of zero.
- Manipulating algebraic expressions: Simplifying, expanding, or factoring expressions.
- Equations with two variables: Exploring relationships between multiple variables.

Each of these topics can be mastered with a systematic approach, practice, and a strong grasp of foundational principles. At its core, algebra uses symbols (variables) to represent numbers. These variables can stand in for unknown quantities, enabling us to express problems in a flexible and structured way. For example, the equation $x+3=5$ asks us to determine which number, when added to 3, equals 5. The solution? $x=2$. This simple problem demonstrates how algebra transforms questions into solvable equations.

But algebra doesn't stop there. Consider the formula $d=r\times t$, where d represents distance, r is the rate (speed), and t is time. This equation captures the relationship between these variables, showing the power of algebra to model real-world scenarios like planning a road trip or calculating the cost of an hourly service.

Algebraic Operations

Algebra relies on the same basic operations as arithmetic—addition, subtraction, multiplication, and division—but with an added layer of abstraction. Instead of fixed numbers, variables bring flexibility to equations:

- **Sum of two numbers**: a+b
- **Difference of two numbers**: a−b
- **Product of two numbers**: a·b or ab
- **Quotient of two numbers**: a/b

These operations form the building blocks of algebra, creating a framework for solving equations and analyzing patterns.

Solving Equations: Step by Step

Solving an equation is like balancing a scale: whatever you do to one side, you must also do to the other. This balance ensures that the equation remains true. Let's break down three examples:

Example 1: Combine Like Terms

3x+4x= 14

- Combine 3x and 4x: 7x= 147
- Divide by 7: x= 2

Example 2: Variables on Both Sides

6x = 4x+8

- Subtract 4x4x4x from both sides: 2x = 8
- Divide by 2: x = 4

Example 3: Rearranging Terms

4x+5 = 2x−3

- Subtract 2x: 2x+5= −3
- Subtract 5: 2x= −8
- Divide by 2: x= −4

Checking Your Work

Always verify your solution by substituting the value of xxx back into the original equation. For example, in 4x+5 = 2x−3, substituting x= −4 gives:

$$4(-4)+5 = 2(-4)-3$$

$$-16+5 = -8-3$$

$$-11 = -11 \checkmark$$

This confirmation ensures your solution is accurate.

Algebraic Inverses			
Operations	Inverse	Operations	Inverse
Addition	Subtraction	Subtraction	Addition
Multiplication	Division	Division	Multiplication
Square	Square Root	Square Root[1]	Square

Positive and Negative Numbers

Positive and negative numbers, often called signed numbers, are foundational elements of mathematics. They're not just abstract concepts—they represent real-world phenomena, like temperatures, financial gains or losses, and elevations above or below sea level.

Visualizing the Number Line

Picture a straight line with zero at the center:

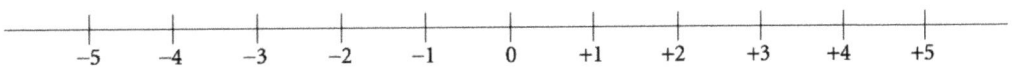

- **Numbers to the right of 0** are positive (e.g., +1, +2, +3).
- **Numbers to the left of 0** are negative (e.g., −1, −2, −3).
- **Zero** is neutral—it's neither positive nor negative.

Positive numbers grow larger as you move to the right, while negative numbers decrease in value as you move further left. For example, −5 is smaller than −2, even though its absolute value (distance from zero) is larger.

Comparisons on the Number Line

Comparing positive and negative numbers is simple when visualized on the number line. A number further to the right is always greater than one to the left:

- 4 > −2 (4 is greater than −2).
- −3 < 1 (−3 is less than 1).

These comparisons allow us to interpret relationships like debts versus savings or temperatures above and below freezing.

Arithmetic with Positive and Negative Numbers

Performing operations with signed numbers might seem tricky at first, but it follows straightforward rules:

Addition:

- **Same signs**: Add the absolute values and keep the sign.
  Example: −3+(−4)= −7
- **Different signs**: Subtract the smaller absolute value from the larger and keep the sign of the larger.
  Example: 5+(−3)= 2

Subtraction: Subtracting is equivalent to adding the opposite.

- Example: 7−(−3) = 7+3= 10

Multiplication and Division:

- **Same signs**: The result is positive.
  Example: (−3)×(−2)= 6
- **Different signs**: The result is negative.
  Example: 4÷(−2)= −2

Order of Operations: "PEMDAS"

When working with multiple operations, follow this sequence:

1. **Parentheses**
2. **Exponents**
3. **Multiplication and Division** (left to right)
4. **Addition and Subtraction** (left to right)

For example, in 2+3×(−4):

- Multiply first: 3×−4= −12
- Then add: 2+(−12)= −10

Remembering **"Please Excuse My Dear Aunt Sally"** ensures you perform calculations in the correct order every time.

Solving Equations with Signed Numbers

When solving equations with positive and negative numbers, the steps are the same as for positive numbers—just keep the sign rules in mind.

Example: Solve −14x+2= 5

1. Subtract 2 from both sides: –14x= 3
2. Divide both sides by –14

$$x = \frac{3}{-14} = -\frac{3}{14}$$

Even with signed numbers, the balance of the equation remains intact as long as you follow the rules step by step.

OPERATION	RULE	EXAMPLE
Addition	If both numbers have the same sign, add them. The answer has the same sign as the numbers being added.	3 + 5= 8 –3 + (–5)= –8
	If both numbers have different signs, subtract the smaller number from the larger. The answer has the same sign as the larger number.	–3 + 5= 2 3 + (–5)= –2
	If both numbers are the same but have opposite signs, the sum is zero.	3 + (–3)= 0
Subtraction	To subtract one number from another, change the sign of the number to be subtracted and then add as above.	3-5 2 = 3 + (–5) = –2 –3-5= –3 + (–5)= –8 –3-(–5)= –3 + 5= 2
Multiplication	Multiply the numbers together. If both numbers have the same sign, the answer is positive; otherwise, it is negative.	3 × 5= 15 –3 × (–5)= 15 –3 × 5= –15 3 × (–5)= –15
	If one number is zero, the answer is zero.	3 × 0= 0
Division	Divide the numbers. If both numbers have the same sign, the answer is positive; otherwise, it is negative.	15 ÷ 3= 5 –15 ÷ (–3)= 5 15 ÷ (–3)= –5 –15 ÷ 3= –5
	If the top number is zero, the answer is zero.	0 ÷ 3= 0

Squares and Square Roots

Mastering squares and square roots is a foundational skill in mathematics, particularly when dealing with geometric concepts like right triangles (think Pythagorean Theorem).

Squaring a number is like multiplying it by itself. For instance, the square of 5 is 25, as 5 multiplied by 5 equals 25. Mathematically, we represent this as:

$5^2 = 25$

Finding the square root of a number is like asking, "What number, when multiplied by itself, gives me this number?" So, the square root of 25 is 5 because 5 times 5 equals 25. We express this as:

$\sqrt{25} = 5$

Common Squares and Square Roots

Square	Value	Square Root	Value
1^2	1	$\sqrt{1}$	1
2^2	4	$\sqrt{4}$	2
3^2	9	$\sqrt{9}$	3
4^2	16	$\sqrt{16}$	4
5^2	25	$\sqrt{25}$	5
6^2	36	$\sqrt{36}$	6
7^2	49	$\sqrt{49}$	7
8^2	64	$\sqrt{64}$	8
9^2	81	$\sqrt{81}$	9
10^2	100	$\sqrt{100}$	10

11^2	121	$\sqrt{121}$	11
12^2	144	$\sqrt{144}$	12
13^2	169	$\sqrt{169}$	13
14^2	196	$\sqrt{196}$	14
15^2	225	$\sqrt{225}$	15
20^2	400	$\sqrt{400}$	20

When you square a number, whether it's positive or negative, the result is always positive. For example, (−3) squared equals 9. However, things get trickier when you try to find the square root of a negative number. In basic arithmetic, the square root of −4 is undefined. This concept introduces us to imaginary numbers, which we won't delve into here.

Evaluating Algebraic Expressions

An algebraic expression is like a mathematical puzzle with letters (called variables) standing in for unknown numbers. For example, 3x-2y means "three times some number (x) minus two times another number (y)."

To solve these puzzles, we replace the letters with their actual values. So, if x is 5 and y is 4 in the expression 3x-2y, we get:

$$3(5)-2(4) = 15-8 = 7$$

Simplifying Algebraic Expressions

Suppose you have a basket of apples and oranges. You can easily combine all the apples together and all the oranges together. Similarly, in algebra, we can group together terms that have the same variables raised to the same power. These are called "like terms."

For example:

- 3x and 4x are like terms because they both have the variable "x."
- 2ab and 7ab are like terms because they both have the variables "a" and "b."
- $3x^2$ and $21x^2$ are like terms because they both have the variable "x" squared.

Let's simplify the expression 3x + 4y - x + 5y:

1. Combine the "x" terms: 3x - x = 2x
2. Combine the "y" terms: 4y + 5y = 9y

So, the simplified expression is 2x + 9y.

Combining Algebraic Expressions

Combining expressions is like adding or subtracting different baskets of fruit. You can only combine the apples with apples and the oranges with oranges.

For example, to add $(5ab - 7ab^2 + 3a^2b) + (9ab - a^2b)$:

1. Combine the "ab" terms: 5ab + 9ab = 14ab
2. Combine the "a^2b" terms: $3a^2b - a^2b = 2a^2b$

The combined expression is $14ab - 7ab^2 + 2a^2b$.

Subtracting Algebraic Expressions

Subtracting expressions is like taking away fruit from a basket. Remember that subtracting is the same as adding the opposite.

For example, to subtract $(3x^2 + 4x - 4) - (x^2 - 3x + 7)$:

1. Change the subtraction sign to addition and flip the signs within the second parentheses: $(3x^2 + 4x - 4) + (-x^2 + 3x - 7)$
2. Combine the "x^2" terms: $3x^2 - x^2 = 2x^2$
3. Combine the "x" terms: $4x + 3x = 7x$
4. Combine the constant terms: $-4 - 7 = -11$

The result is $2x^2 + 7x - 11$.

Multiplying Algebraic Expressions

The key to successfully multiplying algebraic expressions lies in understanding how exponents work.

Exponents: An exponent is a small number written above and to the right of another number or variable. It tells you how many times to multiply that number or variable by itself.

For example:

- $3^2 = 3 \times 3 = 9$
- $y^3 = y \times y \times y$

Rules for Multiplying and Dividing with Exponents:

- **Multiplication:** When multiplying variables with exponents, you add the exponents.
    - Example: $(y^2) \times (y^3) = (y \times y) \times (y \times y \times y) = y^{2+3} = y^5$
- **Division:** When dividing variables with exponents, you subtract the exponents.

    - Example: $y^5 \div y^2 = y^{5-2} = y^3$
    - Example: $x^5 \div x^3 = x^{5-3} = x^2$

Multiplying Terms with Multiple Variables and Numbers:

To multiply expressions with different variables and numbers:

1. Multiply the numbers together.
2. Multiply the variables with the same base by adding their exponents.

Example:

Multiply $(4x^2y^3)(7x^4y^6)$

1. Multiply the numbers: $4 \times 7 = 28$
2. Multiply the "x" terms: $x^2 \times x^4 = x^{2+4} = x^6$
3. Multiply the "y" terms: $y^3 \times y^6 = y^{3+6} = y^9$

Therefore, $(4x^2y^3)(7x^4y^6) = 28x^6y^9$

Multiplying by a Binomial

When multiplying a term by a binomial (an expression with two terms), you need to distribute the term to each part of the binomial. Think of it like sharing the term with both parts inside the parentheses.

For example, if you have $6(x + y)$, it means you're multiplying 6 by both x and y: 6 * x + 6 * y, which equals $6x + 6y$.

Example 1: Multiply $4x(2x^2 + 7x)$

1. **Multiply 4x by $2x^2$:** $4x * 2x^2 = 8x^3$ (Remember to add the exponents of x: $x^1 * x^2 = x^3$)
2. **Multiply 4x by 7x:** $4x * 7x = 28x^2$ (Again, add the exponents: $x^1 * x^1 = x^2$)
3. **Combine the results:** $8x^3 + 28x^2$

Example 2: Multiply $6x^2y^3(4xy + 8xy^2)$

1. **Multiply $6x^2y^3$ by $4xy$:** $6x^2y^3 * 4xy = 24x^3y^4$ (Multiply the numbers and add the exponents of each variable)
2. **Multiply $6x^2y^3$ by $8xy^2$:** $6x^2y^3 * 8xy^2 = 48x^3y^5$
3. **Combine the results:** $24x^3y^4 + 48x^3y^5$

Dividing Algebraic Expressions

When dividing algebraic expressions, follow these steps:

1. **Divide the numbers:** Divide the coefficients (the numbers in front of the variables).
2. **Divide the variables:** Divide the variables with the same base by subtracting their exponents.

Example 1:

Divide $(9x^2) / (3x)$

1. Divide the numbers: $9 / 3 = 3$
2. Divide the "x" terms: $x^2 / x = x^{2-1} = x^1 = x$

Therefore, $(9x^2) / (3x) = 3x$

Example 2:

Divide $(18a^2b^5) / (6ab^2)$

1. Divide the numbers: $18 / 6 = 3$
2. Divide the "a" terms: $a^2 / a = a^{2-1} = a^1 = a$
3. Divide the "b" terms: $b^5 / b^2 = b^{5-2} = b^3$

Therefore, $(18a^2b^5) / (6ab^2) = 3ab^3$

Dividing with Binomials

When dividing an expression with multiple terms by another expression, you must divide each term in the numerator by the denominator.

Example:

Divide $(4x^2y^2 - 8x^3y^2) / (4xy)$

1. **Divide the first term:** $4x^2y^2 / 4xy = (4/4) * (x^2/x) * (y^2/y) = 1 * x * y = xy$
2. **Divide the second term:** $-8x^3y^2 / 4xy = (-8/4) * (x^3/x) * (y^2/y) = -2 * x^2 * y = -2x^2y$

Therefore, $(4x^2y^2 - 8x^3y^2) / (4xy) = xy - 2x^2y$

Equations with Two Variables

An equation with two variables involves two unknown values, typically represented by letters like x and y. For example, $3x + 2y = 6$ is an equation with two variables.

To find a solution to an equation with two variables, you need to find values for x and y that make the equation true. These values must make both sides of the equation equal to each other.

- **Example:** In the equation $3x + 2y = 6$:
    - If $x = 4$ and $y = -3$, then $3(4) + 2(-3) = 12 - 6 = 6$ (The equation is true)
    - If $x = 2$ and $y = 0$, then $3(2) + 2(0) = 6 + 0 = 6$ (The equation is true)
    - If $x = 0$ and $y = 3$, then $3(0) + 2(3) = 0 + 6 = 6$ (The equation is true)

A solution to an equation with two variables is often represented as an **ordered**

pair. An ordered pair is written as (x, y), where x is the value for the first variable and y is the value for the second variable.

- **Example:** (4, –3) is an ordered pair representing the solution where x = 4 and y = –3.

To check if an ordered pair is a solution to an equation, substitute the x and y values into the equation and see if both sides are equal.

- **Example:** (1, 2) is a solution to the equation 3x + y = 5 because:
    - Substituting x = 1 and y = 2: 3(1) + 2 = 3 + 2 = 5

Equation of a Line

An equation like 2x + y = 8 represents a straight line when graphed on a coordinate plane (with x and y axes). This means that all the points that satisfy this equation will lie on the same line.

To determine if a given line matches a particular equation, you can check if the coordinates of points on the line satisfy the equation.

- **Example:** If a line passes through points A(2, 4) and B(3, 2), and the equation is 2x + y = 8:
    - For point A: 2(2) + 4 = 4 + 4 = 8 (The equation is satisfied)
    - For point B: 2(3) + 2 = 6 + 2 = 8 (The equation is satisfied)

Therefore, the line likely has the equation 2x + y = 8.

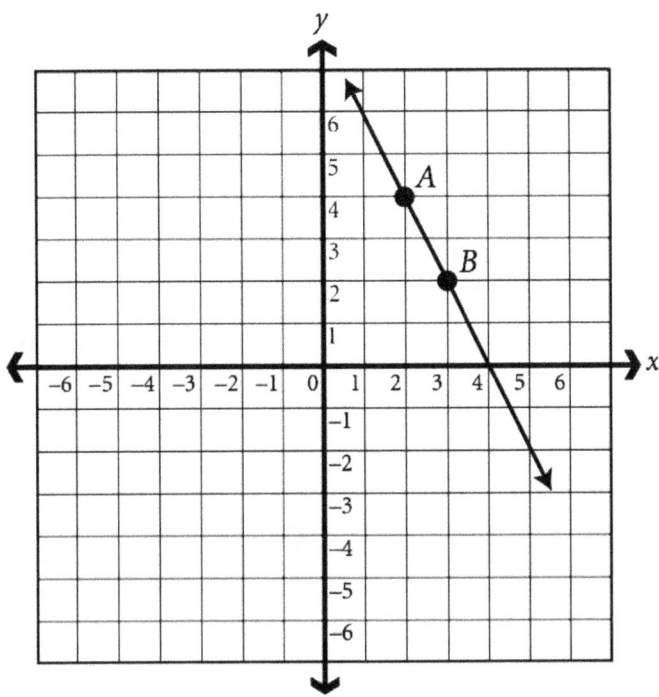

To find the equation of a line from its graph, you can use the coordinates of two points on the line. It's often easiest to use the **intercepts**, which are the points where the line crosses the x-axis and the y-axis.

- **Example:**

    o Let's say a line passes through points A (0, −4) and B (3, 0).
    o To find the correct equation, you would substitute the x and y values of these points into each of the given equations (like a, b, and c in the example).
    o The equation that holds true for both points A and B is the correct equation of the line.

Example: Which of the following represents the equation of the line seen in the graph?

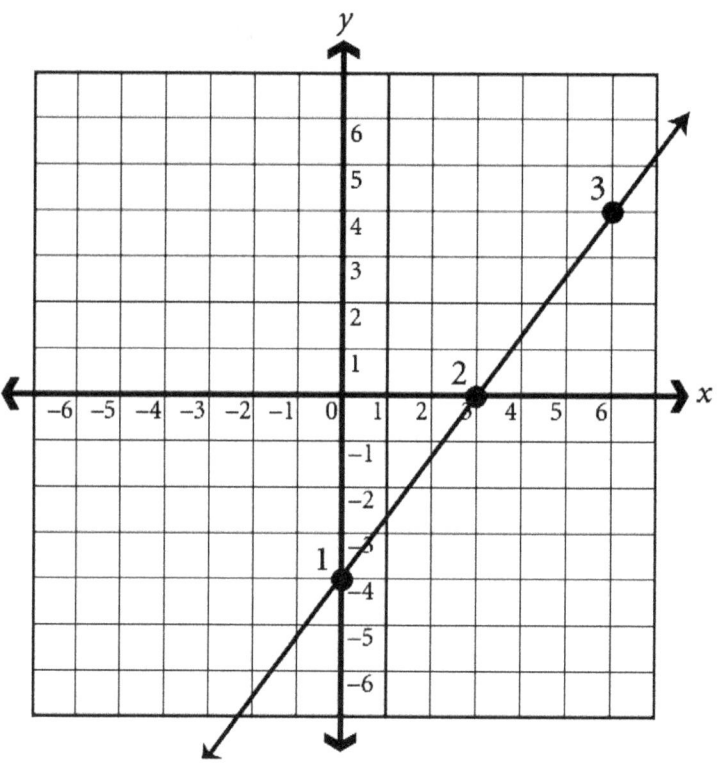

a. x + y = 8
b. 2x + y = 4
c. 4x − 3y = 12

To determine the correct equation for a line, we need to substitute the coordinates of points on the line into each of the given equations.

Let's use two points on the line:

- Point 1 (x = 0, y = −4)
- Point 2 (x = 3, y = 0)

These points are called **intercepts** because they lie on the x-axis and y-axis, respectively.

Now, let's test each equation:

- **Equation a. x + y = 8**

    o   For point 1: 0 + (−4) = −4 ≠ 8
    o   For point 2: 3 + 0 = 3 ≠ 8
    o   This equation doesn't hold true for either point.

- **Equation b. 2x + y = 4**

    o   For point 1: 2(0) + (−4) = −4 ≠ 4
    o   For point 2: 2(3) + 0 = 6 ≠ 4
    o   This equation also doesn't hold true.

- **Equation c. 4x - 3y = 12**

    o   For point 1: 4(0) - 3(−4) = 0 + 12 = 12 (True)
    o   For point 2: 4(3) - 3(0) = 12 - 0 = 12 (True)
    o   This equation is satisfied by both points.

Therefore, the correct equation of the line is **c. 4x - 3y = 12**.

Systems of Equations

A system of equations consists of two or more equations with the same set of variables (usually x and y). A solution to a system of equations is a set of values for the variables that makes all the equations in the system true simultaneously.

To determine if a pair of numbers (x, y) is a solution to a system of equations, you substitute the values of x and y into each equation and check if the equations hold true.

Example 1:

Is (2, 3) a solution to the following system of equations?

- Equation 1: 2x + 3y = 13

- Equation 2: x - y = -1

1. **Substitute x = 2 and y = 3 into Equation 1:** 2(2) + 3(3) = 4 + 9 = 13 This equation holds true.
2. **Substitute x = 2 and y = 3 into Equation 2:** 2 - 3 = -1 This equation also holds true.

Since (2, 3) satisfies both equations, it is a solution to the system of equations.

Example 2:

Is (1, 2) a solution to the following system of equations?

- Equation 1: x + 3y = 7
- Equation 2: 4x + 3y = 7

1. **Substitute x = 1 and y = 2 into Equation 1:** 1 + 3(2) = 1 + 6 = 7 This equation holds true.
2. **Substitute x = 1 and y = 2 into Equation 2:** 4(1) + 3(2) = 4 + 6 = 10 ≠ 7 This equation does not hold true.

Since (1, 2) only satisfies one of the equations, it is not a solution to the system of equations.

Perimeter, Area, and the Pythagorean Theorem

The math exam will include a few questions regarding the Pythagorean Theorem as well as questions about the area and perimeter of quadrilaterals and circles.

Perimeter and Its Practical Applications

Perimeter is a concept that may seem simple at first glance but holds great value in both mathematics and real-world scenarios. It refers to the **distance around a polygon,** or more simply, the total length of the boundary that encloses a shape. The term "perimeter" is derived from the Greek words *peri* (around) and *meter* (measure), meaning "the measurement around." It's easy to see how this definition connects with practical situations, where knowing the perimeter helps us calculate necessary materials or space in everyday life.

To find the perimeter of a polygon, all you need to do is add the lengths of its sides. Whether the shape is a triangle, rectangle, or any other polygon, the formula is simple and direct.

Example:

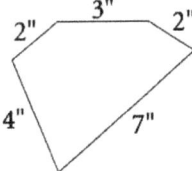

For a polygon with side lengths of 2", 3", 2", 4", and 7", the perimeter is found by adding the sides together:

$$2+3+2+4+7 = 18 \text{ inches}$$

Thus, the perimeter of this polygon is 18 inches.

Perimeter is not just a theoretical concept; it's widely used in real-life situations. Carpenters measure the perimeter of rooms to determine how much ceiling molding is needed. Similarly, a farmer measures the perimeter of a field to calculate how much fencing is required to enclose it. Whether you're building a garden, enclosing a yard, or hanging wallpaper, understanding perimeter helps you plan and execute tasks efficiently.

Example of Perimeter Application:

1. Maryellen's Garden

Maryellen has cleared a 10-foot by 6-foot rectangular plot for her herb garden. She needs to completely enclose it with a chain-link fence, excluding a 3-foot gate. To find the perimeter of the plot, we add the lengths of the sides, but subtract the gate's 3-foot width:

$$(2\times10)+(2\times6)-3 = 20+12-3= 29 \text{ feet}$$

Thus, Maryellen will need 29 feet of fencing to enclose her garden.

2. Terri's Wallpaper Border

Terri plans to hang wallpaper along the top of each wall in her square dressing room. Each wall is 8 feet long, and the wallpaper is sold in 12-foot strips. To find how many strips she needs, we calculate the perimeter of the room and divide by the length of each strip:

$$4\times8= 32 \text{ feet (the perimeter of the square room)}$$

$$32 / 12 \approx 2.67$$

Since Terri cannot purchase a fraction of a strip, she will need to buy 3 strips of wallpaper to cover the perimeter of her dressing room.

Perimeter of a Circle: Circumference

While most polygons have straight sides, circles are a bit different. The perimeter of a circle is called its circumference. The circumference is the total distance around the circle, and it can be calculated using the formula:

$$C=2\pi r$$

Where r is the radius of the circle, and π\pi is approximately 3.14159. Understanding how to calculate the circumference is crucial for tasks such as determining the length of materials needed to enclose a circular space.

Understanding Area

Just as perimeter helps us measure the boundary of a shape, area measures the amount of space that a shape occupies. A square with side lengths of 1 unit covers an area of 1 square unit. The unit of measurement for area varies depending on the context: square feet, square meters, or even square miles.

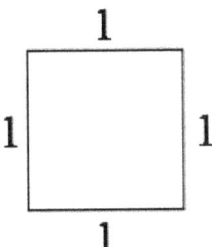

While finding the perimeter is often a matter of adding up the sides, calculating the area of irregular shapes can be more challenging. Sometimes we rely on specific formulas to make the process easier and more accurate. The area of a rectangle is found using the formula:

$$A = \text{length} \times \text{width}$$

In contrast to the perimeter, which measures the boundary, the area tells us how much space is inside the shape.

Quadrilateral

Quadrilaterals are a fundamental concept in geometry, defined as four-sided polygons. Among the many types of quadrilaterals, the rectangle and square are the most commonly encountered in math problems. These shapes share key properties:

- Opposite sides are equal in length and parallel.
- Opposite angles are equal in measure.

Rectangle

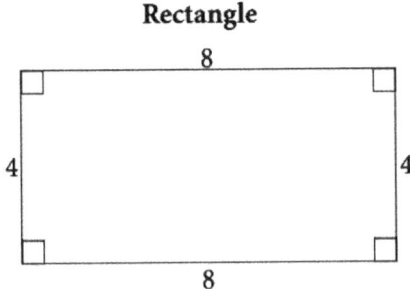

Square

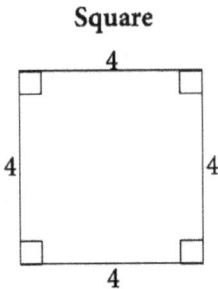

The perimeter of a quadrilateral is the total length of all four sides. For rectangles and squares, shortcuts simplify the calculation:

- Rectangle: Add the lengths of two adjacent sides, then double the sum.
- Square: Multiply the length of one side by four.

Example:

- A square room has a perimeter of 58 feet. To find the length of one side:

$$\text{Side length} = \text{Perimeter}/4 = 58/4 = 14.5 \text{ feet}$$

- A rectangle has a perimeter of 16 feet, with the longer side being three times the shorter side. Let the shorter side be x:

$$2(x+3x) = 16 \rightarrow 8x = 16 \rightarrow x = 2$$

Dimensions: **2 feet by 6 feet**.

The **area** of a quadrilateral measures the space it covers and is expressed in square units. The formulas for area are:

- **Rectangle**: Area = base×height
- **Square**: Area = side^2

Example:

Find the area of a rectangle with a base of 4 meters and height of 3 meters:

$$\text{Area} = 4 \times 3 = 12 \text{ square meters}$$

Real-World Application:

- Tristan is tiling a kitchen floor that measures 15 feet by 18 feet with tiles measuring 12 inches by 18 inches. First, convert all measurements to the same unit:

Kitchen area: 15×18= 270 square feet

Tile area: 1×1.5= 1.5 square feet

$$\text{Number of tiles needed} = \frac{\text{Kitchen area}}{\text{Tile area}} = \frac{270}{1.5} = 180$$

Circles

A **Circle** is a set of points equidistant from a center. Key terms include:

- **Radius**: Distance from the center to any point on the circle.
- **Diameter**: Twice the radius.
- **Circumference**: The distance around the circle, similar to perimeter.

Circumference of a Circle:

Here are the two formulas that you might need to use for determining the formula of a circle.

- C= 2πr
- C= πd

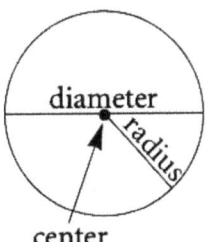

Example 1: Finding Circumference with Radius

1. **Write the formula:** C= 2πr (since we are given the radius)
2. **Substitute the value of the radius:** If the radius is 7 inches, then C= 2*π*7
3. **Calculate:**

    o   If the answer choices include π, then C= 14π inches

o If the answer choices don't include π, substitute π with 3.14 or 22/7 and calculate:

- C = 2 * 3.14 * 7 ≈ 43.96 inches
- C = 2 * (22/7) * 7 = 44 inches

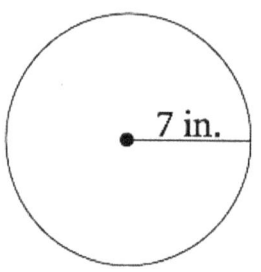

Example 2: Finding Diameter with Circumference

1. **Write the formula:** C= πd
2. **Substitute the given values:** 62.8= 3.14 * d
3. **Solve for d:**

   o Divide both sides by 3.14: 62.8 / 3.14= d
   o d= 20 centimeters

Area of a Circle

The **area** of a circle represents the amount of surface it occupies and is measured in square units, such as square inches, square meters, etc. The formula for calculating the area is:

Area= $πr^2$

Where:

- r is the radius of the circle.
- Π (pi) is approximately equal to 3.14 or 22/7

To avoid mixing up the area and circumference formulas, remember:

- **Area** involves square units (e.g., square inches).
- The area formula includes r^2, while circumference focuses on linear units ($2\pi r$ or πd).

Example 1: Calculating the Area of a Circle

Find the area of a circle with a radius of 2.3 inches, rounded to the nearest tenth.

1. Write the formula: $A = \pi r^2$
2. Substitute $r = 2.3$

$$A = \pi \times 2.3 \times 2.3$$

3. Use $\pi = 3.14$, if the answer doesn't include π:

$$A = 3.14 \times 2.3 \times 2.3 = 16.6 \text{ square inches}$$

4. If the answer includes π\piπ, leave it as:

$$A = 5.3\pi \text{ square inches}$$

Example 2: Finding the Diameter from the Area

A circle has an area of 9π square centimeters. Find its diameter.

1. Write the formula:

$$A = \pi r^2$$

2. Substitute $A = 9\pi$

$$9\pi = \pi r^2$$

3. Simplify:

$$9 = r^2$$

4. Solve for r:

$$r = 9 = 3 \text{ cm}$$

5. The diameter is twice the radius:

$$\text{Diameter} = 2 \times 3 = 6 \text{ cm}$$

The Pythagorean Theorem

The Pythagorean Theorem is a fundamental principle in geometry, used to find the missing side of a right triangle. It states:

$$a^2 + b^2 = c^2$$

Where:

- c is the hypotenuse (the side opposite the right angle, always the longest side).
- a and b are the two shorter sides (legs) of the triangle.

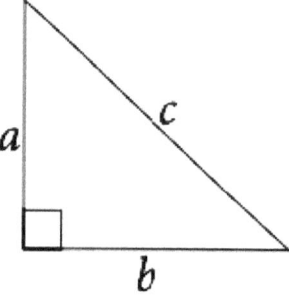

Example: Solving for a Missing Side

Problem: Find the length of the missing side of a triangle with side lengths 3 and 5, where 5 is the hypotenuse.

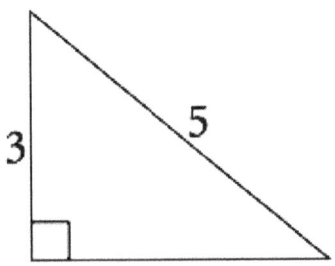

1. Write the formula:

   $$a^2 + b^2 = c^2$$

2. Substitute the known values:

   $$3^2 + b^2 = 5^2$$

3. Simplify the squares:'

   $$9 + b^2 = 25$$

4. Isolate b^2:

   $$b2 = 25 - 9 = 16$$

5. Solve for b by taking the square root:

   $$b = 16 = 4$$

Thus, the missing side has a length of **4 units**.

Here's a real-world problem for you to solve:

Irene is fishing at the edge of a river 40 feet wide, directly across from Sam. Arthur is fishing 30 feet downstream from Sam. How far is Irene from Arthur?

1. Visualize the problem:

    o Irene to Sam forms one leg (a= 40a = 40a= 40 feet).

- o Sam to Arthur forms the other leg (b= 30b = 30b= 30 feet).
- o Irene to Arthur is the hypotenuse (c).

2. Use the Pythagorean theorem:

$$a^2+b^2=c^2$$

3. Substitute the values:

$$40^2+30^2=c^2$$

4. Simplify the squares:

$$1600+900=c^2$$

5. Add and solve for c:

$$c^2=2500$$

$$C=\sqrt{2500}=50$$

Solution: Irene is **50 feet** away from Arthur.

Chapter Seven: HSPT Exam 1

Part 1: Verbal Skills

Time: 16 minutes

1. Which word does NOT belong with the others?

    A. bed
    B. curtains
    C. dresser
    D. armoire

2. Which word does NOT belong with the others?

    A. paper
    B. brick
    C. steel
    D. wood

3. Walnuts cost more than peanuts. Walnuts cost less than pistachios. Pistachios cost more than both peanuts and walnuts. If the first two statements are true, the third is

    A. true
    B. false

C. uncertain
D. repetitive

4. Window is to pane as book is to

   A. novel
   B. glass
   C. cover
   D. page

5. Cup is to gallon as centimeter is to

   A. yard
   B. meter
   C. pint
   D. inch

6. Mutable most nearly means

   A. intangible
   B. secluded
   C. impalpable
   D. inconstant

7. A perceptible change is

   A. recognizable
   B. grandiose
   C. strange
   D. small

8. Which word does NOT belong with the others?

   A. unfortunate
   B. sorrowful
   C. unlucky
   D. regrettable

9. Virtue is the opposite of

   A. reality
   B. wisdom
   C. vice
   D. fact

10. Rodent is to mouse as tree is to

    A. leaf
    B. trunk
    C. elm
    D. squirrel

11. Elated is to despondent as enlightened is to

    A. aware
    B. ignorant
    C. miserable
    D. tolerant

12. Curmudgeonly most nearly means

    A. difficult
    B. striking
    C. powerful
    D. canine

13. A rigorous schedule is

    A. demanding
    B. tolerable
    C. dangerous
    D. orderly

14. All of Joshua's white socks are 100% cotton. Joshua's blue socks are not 100% cotton. All of Joshua's socks are either white or blue. If the first two statements are true, the third is

    A. true
    B. false
    C. uncertain
    D. repetitive

15. Which word does NOT belong with the others?

    A. geology
    B. zoology
    C. theology
    D. botany

16. Which word does NOT belong with the others?

    A. isosceles
    B. equilateral
    C. quadrilateral
    D. scalene

17. The Shop-and-Save Grocery is south of Greenwood Pharmacy. Rebecca's house is northeast of Greenwood Pharmacy. Rebecca's house is west of the Shop-and-Save Grocery. If the first two statements are true, the third is

    A. true
    B. false
    C. uncertain
    D. repetitive

18. Embarrassed is to humiliated as frightened is to

    A. terrified
    B. agitated
    C. courageous

D. reckless

19. Exhaustive is the opposite of

    A. thorough
    B. cursory
    C. tired
    D. energetic

20. Odometer is to mileage as compass is to

    A. speed
    B. hiking
    C. needle
    D. direction

21. Domain most nearly means

    A. entrance
    B. rebellion
    C. formation
    D. territory

22. Escalate most nearly means

    A. intensify
    B. inaugurate
    C. justify
    D. terminate

23. Whiskers weigh less than Paws. Whiskers weigh more than Tabby. Of the three cats, Tabby weighs the least. If the first two statements are true, the third is

    A. true
    B. false
    C. uncertain
    D. repetitive

24. All of Harriet's plants are flowering plants. Some of Harriet's plants are succulents. All succulents are flowering plants. If the first two statements are true, the third is

    A. true
    B. false
    C. uncertain
    D. repetitive

25. Which word does NOT belong with the others?

    A. pecan
    B. walnut
    C. kernel
    D. cashew

26. Which word does NOT belong with the others?

    A. instruct
    B. teach
    C. educate
    D. discipline

27. Innocuous means the opposite of

    A. harmful
    B. inoffensive
    C. incubate
    D. passive

28. Intermittent means the opposite of

    A. repetitive
    B. constant
    C. irregular
    D. staccato

29. Optimist is to cheerful as pessimist is to

   A. gloomy
   B. malicious
   C. petty
   D. benevolent

30. Which word does NOT belong with the others?

   A. roof
   B. sidewalk
   C. door
   D. window

31. A detrimental activity is

   A. decisive
   B. harmful
   C. worthless.
   D. advantageous

32. Placid most nearly means

   A. peaceful
   B. flabby
   C. wise
   D. obedient

33. All Lamels are Signots with buttons. No yellow Signots have buttons. No Lamels are yellow. If the first two statements are true, the third statement is

   A. true
   B. false
   C. uncertain
   D. repetitive

34. Demolish means the opposite of

    A. attend
    B. consider
    C. create
    D. stifle

35. Notable means the opposite of

    A. oral
    B. graceful
    C. legal
    D. ordinary

36. City A has a higher population than City B. City C has a lower population than City B. City A has a lower population than City C. If the first two statements are true, the third statement is

    A. true
    B. false
    C. uncertain
    D. repetitive

37. Which word does NOT belong with the others?

    A. sardine
    B. trout
    C. lobster
    D. catfish

38. Synopsis most nearly means

    A. summary
    B. abundance
    C. stereotype
    D. verification

39. **39.** Methodical most nearly means

    A. erratic
    B. deliberate
    C. humble
    D. deformed

40. Which word does NOT belong with the others?

    A. scythe
    B. knife
    C. pliers
    D. saw

41. Sponge is to porous as rubber is to

    A. massive
    B. solid
    C. elastic
    D. inflexible

42. Martina is sitting at the desk behind Jerome. Jerome is sitting at the desk behind Bryant. Bryant is sitting at the desk behind Martina. If the first two statements are true, the third is

    A. true
    B. false
    C. uncertain
    D. repetitive

43. Which word does NOT belong with the others?

    A. two
    B. three
    C. six
    D. eight

44. Optimum is the opposite of

    A. mediocre.
    B. victorious.
    C. worst.
    D. rational.

45. Candid is to indirect as honest is to

    A. frank.
    B. wicked.
    C. truthful.
    D. devious.

46. Harmony is the opposite of

    A. noise
    B. brevity
    C. safety
    D. conflict

47. Recluse most nearly means

    A. prophet
    B. fool
    C. intellectual
    D. hermit

48. A novel idea is

    A. new
    B. ideal
    C. opinionated
    D. believable

49. Which word does NOT belong with the others?

    A. peninsula

B. island
C. bay
D. cape

50. Pen is to poet as needle is to

    A. thread
    B. button
    C. sewing
    D. tailor

51. Rationale most nearly means

    A. explanation
    B. regret
    C. denial
    D. anticipation

52. Navigate most nearly means

    A. search
    B. decide
    C. steer
    D. assist

53. On the day the Barton triplets were born, Jenna weighed more than Jason. Jason weighed less than Jasmine. Of the three babies, Jasmine weighed the most. If the first two statements are true, the third statement is

    A. true
    B. false
    C. uncertain
    D. repetitive

54. Which word does NOT belong with the others?

    A. seat
    B. rung

C. wood
D. leg

55. A malicious act is

    A. spiteful
    B. changeable
    C. fearful
    D. dangerous

56. Which word does NOT belong with the others?

    A. a. fair
    B. b. just
    C. c. equitable
    D. d. favorable

57. Which word does NOT belong with the others?

    A. defendant
    B. prosecutor
    C. trial
    D. judge

58. Oat cereal has more fiber than corn cereal but less fiber than bran cereal. Corn cereal has more fiber than rice cereal but less fiber than wheat cereal. Rice cereal has the least amount of fiber. If the first two statements are true, the third statement is

    A. true
    B. false
    C. uncertain
    D. repetitive.

59. Which word does NOT belong with the others?

    A. smile

B. feel
C. laugh
D. cry

60. Disperse means the opposite of

   A. gather
   B. agree
   C. praise
   D. satisfy

Part 2: Quantitative Skills

Time: 30 minutes

1. What number is 10% of 60 divided by 2?

   A. 3
   B. 12
   C. 15
   D. 32

2. Look at this series: 44, 44, 50, 50, 56, . . .
   What number should come next?

   A. 44
   B. 48
   C. 56
   D. 62

3. Examine (A), (B), and (C) and find the best answer.

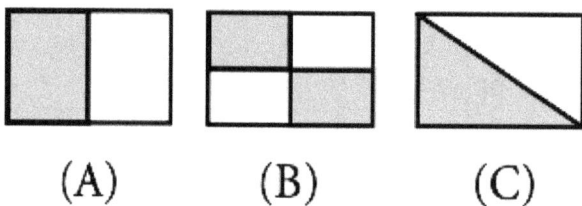

(A)   (B)   (C)

A. (A) is more shaded than (C).
B. (B) is less shaded than (C).
C. (A) is more shaded than (B) but less shaded than (C).
D. (A), (B), and (C) are equally shaded.

4. Examine (A), (B), and (C) and find the best answer.

(A) 3 × (3 + 1)
(B) 1 × (4 + 6)
(C) 2 × (9 + 3)

A. (C) is two times greater than (A).
B. (A) plus 2 is equal to (B).
C. (A) minus (B) is equal to (C).
D. (C) minus (B) is equal to (A).

5. What number is 6 more than 1/2 of 22?

A. 15
B. 17
C. 28
D. 50

6. Examine (A), (B), and (C) and find the best answer.

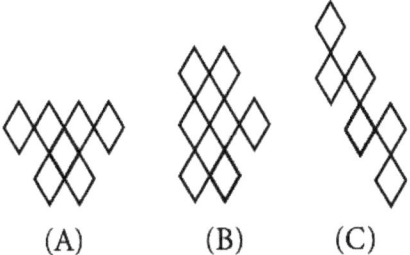

A. (A) has the same number of diamonds as (C) but more diamonds than (B).
B. (B) has more diamonds than (A) or (C).
C. (A) and (B) have the same number of diamonds.
D. (B) and (C) have the same number of diamonds.

7. Look at this series: 50, 5, 40, 10, 30, ...
What number should come next?

   A. 15
   B. 18
   C. 25
   D. 35

8. Examine (A), (B), and (C) and find the best answer.

   (A) 0.5

   (B) 5%

   (C) 1/5

   A. (A) is greater than (B).
   B. (B) is greater than (A).
   C. (C) is greater than (A).
   D. (A) and (B) are equal.

9. Look at this series: 66, 59, 52, 45, 38, ...
What number should come next?

A. 29
B. 31
C. 32
D. 35

10. What number divided by 4 equals 1/2 of 6?

    A. 3
    B. 7
    C. 12
    D. 24

11. What number is 10 more than 25% of 8?

    A. 42
    B. 22
    C. 18
    D. 12

12. Look at this series: 102, 112, 123, 135, ...
    What number should come next?

    A. 146
    B. 148
    C. 150
    D. 152

13. Look at this series: 1/6, 1/3, 1/2, 2/3, ...
    What number should come next?

    A. 1
    B. 4/6
    C. 5/6
    D. 8/9

14. Examine the rectangle and find the best answer.

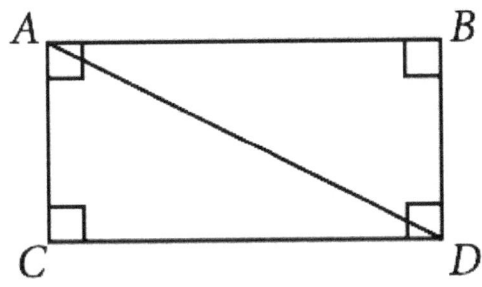

   A. AD is greater than AB.
   B. AD is equal to CD.
   C. AD minus BD is equal to CD.
   D. AB is less than AC.

15. What is six less than 1/9 of 45?

   A. −1
   B. −2
   C. 1
   D. 3

16. Examine (A), (B), and (C) and find the best answer.

   (A) 2/5 of 100
   (B) 1/2 of 80
   (C) 1/8 of 160

   A. (A) is less than (B) or (C).
   B. (A) and (B) are equal.
   C. (B) and (C) are equal.
   D. (B) is greater than (A) but less than (C).

17. Look at this series: V, VIII, XI, XIV, ...
    What number should come next?

    A. IX
    B. XX
    C. XV
    D. XVII

18. What number added to 9 is 6 times 5?

    A. 20
    B. 21
    C. 31
    D. 39

19. Look at this series: 33, 31, 27, 25, 21, ...
    What number should come next?

    A. 17
    B. 19
    C. 20
    D. 24

20. Examine (A), (B), and (C) and find the best answer.

    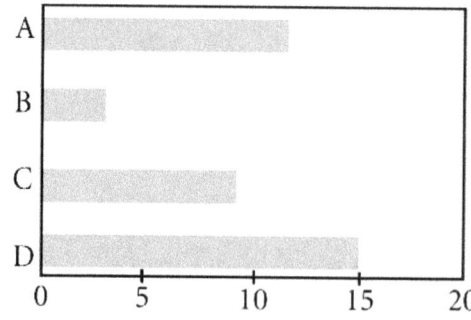

    A. (A) plus (C) is less than (D).
    B. (A) is greater than (D).
    C. (D) minus (B) is equal to (C).

D. (D) is greater than (B) plus (C).

21. What number is 6 less than 2/5 of 25?

    A. −4
    B. 1
    C. 4
    D. 9

22. What number is 3 times 4% of 20?

    A. 2.4
    B. 5.4
    C. 24
    D. 27

23. Examine (A), (B), and (C) and find the best answer.

    A. (A) plus (B) equals (C).
    B. (C) minus (A) equals (B).
    C. (C) is greater than (A) plus (B).
    D. (C) is less than (A) plus (B).

24. Look at this series: 1/9, 1/3, 1, 3, . . .
    What number should come next?

    A. ⅔
    B. 6

C. 9
D. 12

25. Examine (A), (B), and (C) and find the best answer.

    (A) 3% of 100
    (B) 6% of 50
    (C) 12% of 25

    A. (A) is less than (B) or (C).
    B. (C) is greater than (A) or (B).
    C. (B) is less than (C) but greater than (A).
    D. (A), (B), and (C) are all equal.

26. Examine (A), (B), and (C) and find the best answer.

    (A) n × n
    (B) n^2
    (C) n(n)

    A. (A) plus (C) equals (B).
    B. (B) is greater than (C) but less than (A).
    C. (A) is less than (C).
    D. (A), (B), and (C) are all equal.

27. Look at this series: 21, 9, 21, 11, __, 13, ...

    What number should fill the blank?

    A. 12
    B. 15
    C. 21
    D. 23

28. Examine (A), (B), and (C) and find the best answer.

    (A) 7^2

(B) 4^3
(C) $3^2 + 6$

  A. (A) and (B) are equal.
  B. b. (A) is greater than (B).
  C. c. (B) minus (A) is equal to (C).
  D. d. (B) and (C) are equal to (A).

29. Look at this series: 5.2, 4.8, 4.4, 4, ...
 What number should come next?

  A. 3
  B. 3.3
  C. 3.5
  D. 3.6

30. Look at this series: 7, 10, 8, 11, 9, __, 10, . . .
 What number should fill the blank?

  A. 7
  B. 11
  C. 12
  D. 13

31. What number divided by 5 is 1/10 of 300?

  A. 150
  B. 100
  C. 50
  D. 30

32. What number added to 15% of 30 equals 20?

  A. −25
  B. 4.5
  C. 12
  D. 15.5

33. Look at this series: 2, 5, 28, 8, 11, 20, 14, ...
    What number should come next?

    A. 12
    B. 17
    C. 23
    D. 28

34. Examine (A), (B), and (C) and find the best answer.

    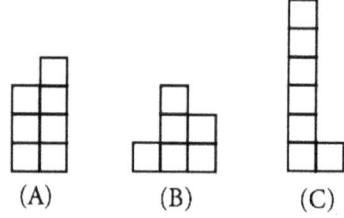

    A. Only (A) and (B) are equal.
    B. Only (A) and (C) are equal.
    C. Only (B) and (C) are equal.
    D. (A), (B), and (C) are all equal.

35. Examine the figure and find the best answer.

    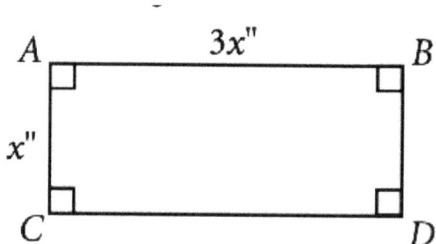

    A. AC plus BD is less than AB.
    B. AB minus CD is equal to AC.
    C. AB minus AC is equal to BD.
    D. AC plus BD is greater than CD.

36. Look at this series: 2, 6, 18, 54, ...
    What number should come next?

A. 108
B. 148
C. 162
D. 216

37. What number plus 2 times the same number equals 99?

    A. 16
    B. 33
    C. 66
    D. 297

38. What number is 16 more than 12% of 1,000?

    A. 1.36
    B. 13.6
    C. 136
    D. 1,360

39. Examine (A), (B), and (C) and find the best answer.

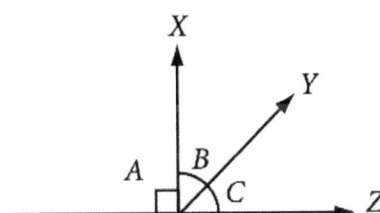

    A. Angle (A) plus angle (B) equals a right angle.
    B. Angle (A) plus angle (B) plus angle (C) equals a right angle.
    C. Angle (B) plus angle (C) equals angle (A).
    D. Angle (A) plus angle (B) equals angle (C).

40. Look at this series: 1,000, 200, 40, ...
    What number should come next?

    A. 8
    B. 10
    C. 15

D. 20

41. Examine (A), (B), and (C) and find the best answer.

   (A) 18
   (B) 6(4 + 1)
   (C) 3(4)

   A. (B) is greater than (C) but less than (A).
   B. (B) divided by (C) is equal to (A).
   C. (C) is greater than (A).
   D. (A) plus (C) is equal to (B).

42. Look at this series: U32, V29, W26, X23, ...
    What number should come next?

    A. Y20
    B. Y17
    C. Z20
    D. Z26

43. Look at this series: 664, 332, 340, 170, 178, ...
    What number should come next?

    A. 89
    B. 94
    C. 109
    D. 184

44. Seven times what number equals 60% of 770 divided by 6?

    A. 7
    B. 11
    C. 12
    D. 110

45. 33 is 12% of what number?

   A. 27.5
   B. 39.6
   C. 185
   D. 275

46. Look at this series: 2, IV, 8, XVI, ...
    What number should come next?

   A. XXXII
   B. XIX
   C. 16
   D. 32

47. Look at this series: 17, __, 28, 28, 39, 39, ...
    What number should fill the blank?

   A. 6
   B. 17
   C. 28
   D. 50

48. Examine (A), (B), and (C) and find the best answer.

   (A) 52 inches
   (B) 1 foot 3 inches
   (C) 1 yard 1 inch

   A. (A) is 3 times greater than (B).
   B. (A) minus (B) is equal to (C).
   C. (A) and (B) are equal.
   D. (A) is less than (C).

49. Examine the circle and find the best answer.

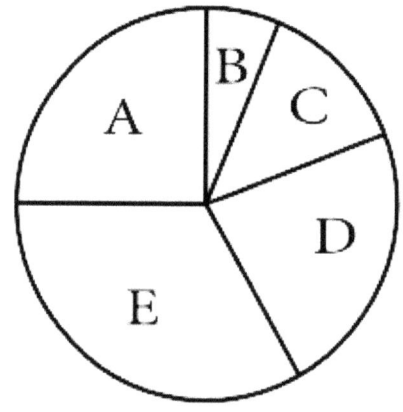

A. B and C are equal to A.
B. E minus A is less than D.
C. B plus C plus D is equal to A plus E.
D. A plus B plus C is equal to D plus E.

50. Look at this series: 75, 65, 85, 55, __, 85, 35, 25, ...
What number should fill the blank?

A. 25
B. 45
C. 65
D. 85

51. What number is 42 less than 1/5 of 820?

A. 98
B. 112
C. 122
D. 210

52. What number divided by 4 is equal to 8 more than 4 times 2?

A. 48
B. 60
C. 64

D. 96

Part 3: Reading Skills

Time: 25 minutes

Passage 1:

For questions 1 through 6, read the following passage carefully. Answer the questions that follow only on the basis of the preceding passage.

The Fascinating World of Bats

Bats are some of the most misunderstood creatures in the animal kingdom. Often associated with darkness and mystery, they play an essential role in maintaining ecological balance. There are over 1,400 species of bats, making them the second-largest order of mammals after rodents. Found in nearly every corner of the world except for extreme deserts and polar regions, bats are incredibly adaptable.

Most bats are nocturnal, which means they are active at night. They use echolocation, a biological sonar, to navigate and hunt in the dark. By emitting high-frequency sound waves and interpreting the returning echoes, bats can locate insects, avoid obstacles, and find their way in total darkness.

Bats are vital to ecosystems because they help control insect populations. A single bat can eat hundreds of mosquitoes in an hour, which benefits humans by reducing the spread of mosquito-borne diseases. Additionally, fruit bats are important pollinators and seed dispersers. Some plants, such as bananas, mangoes, and agave (used to produce tequila), rely heavily on bats for pollination.

Despite their importance, bats face numerous threats, including habitat loss, climate change, and a disease called white-nose syndrome, which has devastated bat populations in North America. Conservationists emphasize the need to protect these animals because of their ecological significance.

Interestingly, many cultures have varying perceptions of bats. In some, they are symbols of good luck and prosperity, while in others, they are linked to fear and superstition. Understanding the true nature of bats helps dispel myths and encourages conservation efforts.

Questions

1. According to the passage, what is the main reason bats are considered important to ecosystems?

    A. They are symbols of good luck.
    B. They eat large amounts of insects.
    C. They live in most parts of the world.
    D. They use echolocation to navigate.

2. What does the term "echolocation" refer to in the passage?

    A. A process of conserving energy during the day.
    B. A biological system that helps bats see in the dark.
    C. A method bats use to locate objects using sound.
    D. A way bats protect themselves from predators.

3. Why are fruit bats important for certain plants?

    A. They help plants grow faster.
    B. They pollinate flowers and disperse seeds.
    C. They keep insects away from plants.
    D. They improve soil quality.

4. What is one major threat mentioned in the passage that bats face?

    A. Overpopulation of insects.
    B. Lack of food in urban areas.
    C. White-nose syndrome.
    D. Excessive hunting by humans.

5. According to the passage, which of the following statements is true?

    A. All bats are active during the day.

    B. Bats can only survive in tropical climates.
    C. Bats help reduce the spread of diseases by eating mosquitoes.
    D. Bats rely on vision rather than sound to find food.

6. What is the main purpose of the passage?

    A. To provide information about bats and their ecological importance.
    B. To warn people about the dangers of bats.
    C. To explain how echolocation works in other animals.
    D. To describe the cultural significance of bats.

Passage 2:

For questions 7 through 12, read the following passage carefully. Answer the questions that follow only on the basis of the preceding passage.

The Hidden World of Coral Reefs

Coral reefs are often called the "rainforests of the sea" because of their incredible biodiversity. They cover less than 1% of the ocean floor but support nearly 25% of all marine species. These underwater ecosystems are made up of coral polyps, tiny animals that form colonies and secrete calcium carbonate to create hard exoskeletons. Over time, these skeletons build up to form the reefs we see today.

Coral reefs are found primarily in warm, shallow waters in tropical and subtropical regions. They thrive in clear, sunlit water because corals have a symbiotic relationship with algae called zooxanthellae. The algae live inside the coral's tissues and perform photosynthesis, providing energy for the coral in exchange for a safe habitat.

Apart from being a home to countless species, coral reefs are vital to humans as well. They protect coastal areas from storm surges and erosion, support fishing industries, and attract millions of tourists annually. Additionally, coral reef organisms are used in medical research to develop treatments for diseases such as cancer and arthritis.

However, coral reefs face numerous threats. Climate change, rising sea temperatures, and ocean acidification have led to coral bleaching, where corals expel the algae living in their tissues, turning white and often dying. Overfishing, pollution, and destructive practices like bottom trawling also contribute to the decline of coral reefs. Conservation efforts, such as marine protected areas and sustainable fishing practices, are critical to preserving these ecosystems for future generations.

Questions

7. Why are coral reefs referred to as the "rainforests of the sea"?

    A. They are found in rainforests.
    B. They support a high diversity of marine life.
    C. They grow at the same rate as rainforests.
    D. They are covered in algae that resemble forests.

8. What is the role of zooxanthellae in coral reefs?

    A. They protect coral reefs from storms.
    B. They provide corals with energy through photosynthesis.
    C. They clean the water surrounding coral reefs.
    D. They help corals grow faster by producing calcium.

9. How do coral reefs benefit humans?

    A. By reducing global warming.
    B. By providing a habitat for large predators.
    C. By protecting coastlines and supporting tourism.
    D. By cleaning pollutants from the water.

10. What is coral bleaching, according to the passage?

    A. The natural growth process of coral reefs.
    B. The process of corals expelling algae and losing color.

C. The damage caused by overfishing and pollution.
D. The effect of calcium carbonate on coral reefs.

11. Which of the following is NOT mentioned as a threat to coral reefs?

    A. Rising sea temperatures.
    B. Ocean acidification.
    C. Marine protected areas.
    D. Destructive fishing practices.

12. What is the main purpose of the passage?

    A. To explain the economic value of coral reefs.
    B. To describe coral reefs and highlight their importance.
    C. To discuss how coral reefs are formed over time.
    D. To list threats to coral reefs and their solutions.

Passage 3:

For questions 13 through 18, read the following passage carefully. Answer the questions that follow only on the basis of the preceding passage.

The Rise of Artificial Intelligence

Artificial Intelligence (AI) is transforming the way we live, work, and interact with the world. At its core, AI refers to machines and computer systems capable of performing tasks that typically require human intelligence. These tasks include problem-solving, decision-making, understanding language, and recognizing patterns. Over the years, advancements in AI have given rise to technologies such as virtual assistants, self-driving cars, and predictive algorithms.

The development of AI can be traced back to the mid-20th century when computer scientists began exploring ways to simulate human thought processes. Today, AI systems are powered by machine learning, a process where computers analyze vast amounts of data to identify patterns and improve their performance over time. For instance, AI algorithms can now analyze medical images to detect diseases like cancer with remarkable accuracy.

AI also plays a significant role in daily life. Virtual assistants like Siri and Alexa use natural language processing (NLP) to understand and respond to voice commands. Online recommendation systems, such as those on Netflix or Amazon, analyze user preferences to suggest movies or products. AI even influences industries like finance, where it detects fraudulent transactions, and education, where it personalized learning experiences for students.

However, the rise of AI is not without challenges. Ethical concerns, such as bias in AI systems and the potential loss of jobs due to automation, have sparked debates worldwide. Additionally, fears surrounding the misuse of AI, such as its application in surveillance or autonomous weapons, underscore the need for regulations to ensure responsible development.

Despite these challenges, AI has the potential to address global problems. From combating climate change by optimizing energy use to improving healthcare access in remote areas, AI offers innovative solutions that were once unimaginable. The key lies in balancing innovation with ethical responsibility to maximize its benefits while minimizing risks.

Questions

13. What is the primary function of artificial intelligence?

    A. To create physical robots.
    B. To perform tasks that require human intelligence.
    C. To replace human jobs entirely.
    D. To develop new computer systems.

14. How do AI systems improve their performance over time?

    A. By simulating human emotions.
    B. Through repeated programming by engineers.
    C. By analyzing large datasets to identify patterns.
    D. Through trial and error without data analysis.

15. Which of the following is NOT mentioned as a use of AI?

    A. Detecting fraudulent financial transactions.
    B. Creating new musical compositions.
    C. Analyzing medical images.
    D. Suggesting movies or products online.

16. Why is the rise of AI considered controversial?

    A. It has no practical applications.
    B. It poses ethical challenges and risks.
    C. It replaces virtual assistants like Siri and Alexa.
    D. It prevents the development of regulations.

17. According to the passage, what is a potential benefit of AI?

    A. Reducing the need for human creativity.
    B. Solving global issues like climate change.
    C. Making all human jobs obsolete.
    D. Eliminating the need for ethical discussions.

18. What is the main message of the passage?

    A. AI is a perfect solution to all modern problems.
    B. AI is dangerous and should be avoided.
    C. AI offers significant benefits but requires ethical oversight.
    D. AI development has no connection to human intelligence.

Passage 4:

For questions 19 through 24, read the following passage carefully. Answer the questions that follow only on the basis of the preceding passage.

The Mystery of Deep Ocean Exploration

Despite covering more than 70% of Earth's surface, the oceans remain one of the least explored regions of our planet. Scientists estimate that more than 80% of the world's oceans are still unmapped, unobserved, and unexplored. While space exploration often captures the public's imagination, the deep ocean holds mysteries that could unlock answers to some of humanity's most pressing questions.

The deep ocean is defined as any part of the ocean below 200 meters, where sunlight no longer penetrates. This region, often referred to as the "midnight zone," is home to unique ecosystems and creatures adapted to survive in extreme conditions. For instance, bioluminescent fish use their glow to attract prey or evade predators, while some organisms thrive near hydrothermal vents, relying on chemical energy instead of sunlight.

Exploring these depths is a challenging task due to immense water pressure, freezing temperatures, and complete darkness. Advanced technologies such as remotely operated vehicles (ROVs), autonomous underwater vehicles (AUVs), and specialized submersibles have allowed scientists to venture into these alien-like environments. These missions have led to remarkable discoveries, including new species and natural resources such as methane hydrates.

The deep ocean is not just a place of scientific curiosity but also of significant importance to our planet's health. Oceans regulate the Earth's climate by absorbing carbon dioxide and distributing heat. Additionally, many pharmaceutical compounds derived from marine organisms show potential for treating diseases like cancer and Alzheimer's.

However, deep ocean exploration faces several hurdles, including high costs, technological limitations, and environmental concerns. Human activities, such as deep-sea mining and plastic pollution, threaten these fragile ecosystems before we fully understand them. Preserving the ocean's biodiversity requires international cooperation and a commitment to sustainable practices.

The deep ocean remains a frontier of discovery, holding secrets that could benefit science, medicine, and environmental conservation. As we dive deeper, we gain not only knowledge but also a renewed responsibility to protect this vital resource.

Questions

19. What percentage of the world's oceans remain unexplored?

    A. 50%
    B. 60%
    C. 70%
    D. 80%

20. What is the "midnight zone"?

    A. The part of the ocean where sunlight no longer reaches.
    B. A region of the ocean with the highest biodiversity.
    C. A nickname for shallow coastal waters.
    D. The surface area of the ocean is visible at night.

21. Which technological tool is used for deep ocean exploration?

    A. Space probes
    B. Remotely operated vehicles (ROVs)
    C. Infrared satellites
    D. Robotic arms for land excavation

22. Why are oceans crucial for regulating Earth's climate?

    A. They produce oxygen through marine algae.
    B. They reflect sunlight away from the planet.
    C. They absorb carbon dioxide and distribute heat.
    D. They prevent volcanic activity on the seafloor.

23. What is one threat to deep ocean ecosystems mentioned in the passage?

    A. Overfishing of surface-dwelling fish.
    B. Increased activity of volcanic vents.
    C. Deep-sea mining and plastic pollution.
    D. The natural extinction of deep-sea organisms.

24. What is the central message of the passage?

   A. Deep ocean exploration is more important than space exploration.
   B. The deep ocean holds untapped potential and needs protection.
   C. Marine organisms are the primary source of new diseases.
   D. The oceans are fully understood and mapped.

Passage 5:

For questions 25 through 32, read the following passage carefully. Answer the questions that follow only on the basis of the preceding passage.

Understanding Fire Safety

Fires can be devastating, but with proper precautions and knowledge, many fire-related accidents can be prevented. Fire safety is not only about reacting to a fire but also about taking steps to minimize risks and ensure the safety of people and property.

A key aspect of fire safety is understanding the fire triangle, which consists of three elements: heat, fuel, and oxygen. A fire needs all three to ignite and sustain itself. Removing any one of these elements will extinguish the fire. For example, water removes heat, while fire extinguishers work by cutting off oxygen or chemically disrupting the reaction.

Smoke alarms are one of the most effective tools for fire prevention in homes. Properly installed and maintained alarms can reduce the risk of death by nearly half. It is recommended to test smoke alarms monthly and replace their batteries at least once a year. Families should also create and practice a fire escape plan, ensuring that all members know at least two ways to exit every room.

Cooking is one of the leading causes of house fires. Never leave food unattended on the stove, and keep flammable items like towels or paper away from heat sources. Similarly, electrical fires can result from overloaded outlets, frayed wires, or malfunctioning appliances. Regular inspections and avoiding the use of damaged equipment can significantly reduce this risk.

In case of a fire, the most important rule is to get out and stay out. Trying to retrieve belongings or fight the fire yourself can lead to severe injuries. Once outside, call emergency services and avoid re-entering the building.

Public spaces, such as schools and offices, are often equipped with fire safety features like sprinkler systems and fire extinguishers. It is essential to familiarize yourself with the fire exits in any building you enter. Knowing where to go in an emergency can save lives.

Fire safety is everyone's responsibility. By staying informed and vigilant, we can protect ourselves, our families, and our communities from the dangers of fire.

Questions

25. What are the three elements of the fire triangle?

    A. Heat, fuel, water
    B. Heat, fuel, oxygen
    C. Fuel, water, oxygen
    D. Fire, smoke, water

26. How often should smoke alarms be tested?

    A. Once a week
    B. Monthly
    C. Every six months
    D. Annually

27. What should you do if a fire breaks out in your home?

    A. Try to extinguish the fire yourself.
    B. Gather valuable belongings before leaving.
    C. Get out and stay out, then call emergency services.
    D. Turn off the electricity and water supply first.

28. What is a common cause of house fires?

    A. Lightning strikes
    B. Unattended cooking
    C. Using too many smoke alarms
    D. Regular appliance inspections

29. Why is it important to know fire exits in public spaces?

    A. To find the quickest way to leave in an emergency.
    B. To locate sprinkler systems during a fire.
    C. To ensure compliance with building codes.
    D. To reduce the risk of electrical fires.

30. What is the central message of the passage?

    A. Fires are inevitable, but they can be managed.
    B. Fire safety requires proactive measures and awareness.
    C. Smoke alarms are the only necessary fire prevention tool.
    D. Fire safety is solely the responsibility of public officials.

31. What should you do to reduce the risk of electrical fires at home?

    A. Avoid overloading outlets and regularly inspect appliances.
    B. Use fire extinguishers near electrical outlets.
    C. Unplug all appliances when not in use.
    D. Install more smoke alarms in each room.

32. Why is it not advisable to try retrieving belongings during a fire?

    A. It can delay emergency services from responding.
    B. It increases the risk of severe injuries or fatalities.
    C. It might cause further damage to the property.
    D. It violates fire safety regulations.

Passage 6:

For questions 31 through 40, read the following passage carefully. Answer the questions that follow only on the basis of the preceding passage.

The Basics of Acupuncture

Acupuncture, an ancient practice rooted in traditional Chinese medicine, has been used for thousands of years to promote health and well-being. It involves the insertion of thin needles into specific points on the body, called acupoints, to stimulate energy flow, or "qi" (pronounced "chee"). This energy is believed to travel through pathways in the body known as meridians, and any blockage or imbalance in qi is thought to cause illness or discomfort.

Modern science has taken an interest in acupuncture, seeking to understand its effects through rigorous studies. While the exact mechanisms are still not fully understood, many researchers suggest that acupuncture stimulates the nervous system, releasing chemicals in the brain and body that help reduce pain and promote relaxation.

Acupuncture is often used to address chronic pain, such as backaches, migraines, and arthritis. Additionally, it has gained popularity as a complementary treatment for stress, anxiety, and insomnia. Many patients report a sense of calm and improved well-being after a session, which typically lasts between 30 minutes and an hour.

The safety of acupuncture largely depends on the skill of the practitioner and the use of sterile needles. Licensed acupuncturists undergo extensive training to ensure they understand both the traditional principles and modern safety standards. The procedure is generally considered safe, with minimal side effects such as mild soreness or bruising at the needle sites.

Though acupuncture is not a cure-all, its ability to complement other treatments has made it a valuable tool in integrative medicine. By combining ancient wisdom with modern understanding, acupuncture continues to bridge the gap between traditional practices and contemporary healthcare.

Questions

33. What is the primary purpose of acupuncture?

    A. To cure all diseases.
    B. To stimulate the flow of energy in the body.
    C. To block nerve signals entirely.
    D. To replace modern medicine.

34. What are meridians, according to traditional Chinese medicine?

    A. Pathways for energy flow in the body.
    B. Specific needle types used in acupuncture.
    C. Bones connected to acupoints.
    D. Points where the nervous system is inactive.

35. Which of the following conditions is acupuncture commonly used to address?

    A. Broken bones
    B. Chronic pain and stress
    C. Digestive infections
    D. Acute viral illnesses

36. What is one possible explanation for how acupuncture works, as suggested by modern science?

    A. It creates permanent changes in DNA.
    B. It removes toxins from the bloodstream.
    C. It stimulates the nervous system and releases chemicals that reduce pain.
    D. It increases the body's production of energy for physical activity.

37. Why is it important for acupuncturists to use sterile needles?

    A. To ensure the needles are sharp enough to penetrate skin.
    B. To prevent infection and maintain patient safety.
    C. To increase the effectiveness of the treatment.
    D. To comply with modern pain relief techniques.

38. What is the main idea of the passage?

    A. Acupuncture is a highly controversial practice with no scientific backing.
    B. Acupuncture is an ancient practice that complements modern healthcare by promoting relaxation and addressing chronic conditions.
    C. Acupuncture should only be practiced in hospitals under strict medical supervision.
    D. Acupuncture is outdated and has been replaced by contemporary treatments.

39. What is a reported benefit of acupuncture for patients beyond addressing physical pain?

    E. Improved digestion
    F. Enhanced energy for physical activity
    G. A sense of calm and improved well-being
    H. Better immunity against infections

40. What does the passage suggest about the role of acupuncture in modern medicine?

    A. It has replaced many contemporary treatments.
    B. It serves as a complementary tool alongside other treatments.
    C. It is only useful for treating chronic illnesses.
    D. It is primarily used for experimental research.

For questions 41 through 60, choose the word or phrase that most nearly means the same as the underlined word.

41. to **aggravate** the situation

    A. worsen
    B. anger
    C. complicate
    D. solve

42. a **tenuous** hold

    A. thin
    B. intense
    C. tender
    D. slight

43. a **sardonic** remark

    A. cynical
    B. fishy
    C. serious
    D. unnecessary

44. a **bucolic** landscape

    A. cow-filled
    B. rustic
    C. happy
    D. urban

45. to **recuperate** fully

    A. recover
    B. endorse
    C. persist
    D. approve

46. a **humble** person

    A. common
    B. tolerant
    C. conceited
    D. meek

47. **articulate** the philosophy

    A. trust
    B. refine
    C. verify
    D. express

48. the **expansive** facility

    A. obsolete
    B. meager
    C. spacious
    D. costly

49. the beautiful **mesa**

    A. woman
    B. plateau
    C. valley
    D. dwelling

50. his **meticulous** examination

    A. delicate
    B. painstaking
    C. responsible
    D. objective

51. his **animosity** toward us

    A. readiness
    B. compassion
    C. hostility
    D. impatience

52. regain your **composure**

    A. status
    B. poise
    C. liveliness
    D. voice

53. a **spurious** statement

    A. prevalent
    B. false
    C. melancholy
    D. actual

54. her **commendable** action

    A. admirable
    B. accountable
    C. irresponsible
    D. noticeable

55. to **emulate** another person

    A. imitate
    B. convince
    C. fascinate
    D. punish

56. the **meager** supply

    A. sincere
    B. abundant
    C. scant
    D. precise

57. a **noxious** odor

    A. floral
    B. pleasant
    C. harmful
    D. strange

58. to have **equity**

    A. justice
    B. certainty
    C. wealth
    D. dread

59. a **jubilant** graduate

    A. charming
    B. joyful
    C. stubborn
    D. scholarly

60. our neighbor's **affluence**

    A. disregard
    B. wealth
    C. greed
    D. shame

Part 4: Mathematics

Time: 45 minutes

1. Write ten thousand four hundred forty-seven in numerals.

    A. 10,499,047
    B. 104,447

C. 10,447
D. 1,047

2. In algebra, a "variable" is

    A. the known quantity in the equation.
    B. a symbol that stands for a number.
    C. an inequality.
    D. the solution for the equation.

3. In the following decimal, which digit is in the hundredths place? 0.9402

    A. 9
    B. 0
    C. 2
    D. 4

4. Which of the following numbers is the smallest?

    A. $6/10$
    B. $8/15$
    C. $33/60$
    D. $11/20$

5. 62.5% is equal to

    A. $1/16$
    B. $5/8$
    C. $6 \frac{1}{4}$
    D. $6 \frac{2}{5}$

6. A straight angle is

    A. exactly 180 degrees.
    B. between 90 and 180 degrees.
    C. 90 degrees.
    D. less than 90 degrees.

7. $(-6)^2 =$

   A. −36
   B. 36
   C. −12
   D. 12

8. What is the result of multiplying 11 by 0.032?

   A. 0.032
   B. 0.0352
   C. 0.32
   D. 0.352

9. **9.** Which of these angle measures forms a right triangle?

   A. 40 degrees, 40 degrees, 100 degrees
   B. 20 degrees, 30 degrees, 130 degrees
   C. 40 degrees, 40 degrees, 40 degrees
   D. 40 degrees, 50 degrees, 90 degrees

10. The ratio of 2 ounces to 1 pound is

    A. 2:1
    B. 1:16
    C. 1:8
    D. 2:8

11. Which of the following is the best simplification of the following sentence?
    Salwa is ten years older than Roland.

    A. 10 + S = R
    B. S + R = 10
    C. R − 10 = S
    D. S = R + 10

12. What is the reciprocal of 3¾?

    A. 4/15
    B. 15/4
    C. 14/5
    D. 5/14

13. What is another way to write 2.75 × 100²?

    A. 275
    B. 2,750
    C. 27,500
    D. 270,000

14. What is the complementary angle to 36 degrees?

    A. 324 degrees
    B. 144 degrees
    C. 54 degrees
    D. 36 degrees

15. Which of the following number sentences is true?

    A. 4 feet > 3 feet
    B. 7 feet < 6 feet
    C. 5 feet > 6 feet
    D. 3 feet < 2 feet

16. Which of the following is true?

    A. 0.008 > 0.08
    B. 1.5 > 1.455
    C. 3.662 > 3.7
    D. 0.5 < 0.09

17. The greatest common factor of 16 and 38 is

    A. 2.
    B. 4.
    C. 8.
    D. 16.

18. A certain quadrilateral has a set of two parallel sides and an angle of 54 degrees. Which of the following could it be?

    A. triangle
    B. rectangle
    C. square
    D. parallelogram

19. In 1995, the number of insects on earth was estimated at 10^{18}. How many insects was that?

    A. 10 × 10 eighteen times
    B. 10 + 18 ten times
    C. 10 million × 18 million
    D. 18 × 18 ten times

20. What is the greatest area possible enclosed by a quadrilateral with a perimeter of 24 feet?

    A. 6 square feet
    B. 24 square feet
    C. 36 square feet
    D. 48 square feet

21. What is 0.3642 rounded to the nearest hundredth?

    A. 0.4
    B. 0.37
    C. 0.364
    D. 0.36

22. Which symbol belongs in the underline?

    0.05 __ 2/5

    A. <
    B. >
    C. =
    D. ≤

23. Which is the greatest?

    A. 6 pints
    B. 3 quarts
    C. 1 gallon
    D. 10 cups

24. What is the difference in perimeter/circumference between a square with a base of 4 feet and a circle with a diameter of 4 feet?

    A. 8 − 2π feet
    B. 16 − 2π feet
    C. 16 − 4π feet
    D. 16 − 8π feet

25. Bill's dog Muffin ate 14 ounces of Hearty Meal dog food and then helped herself to 6 ounces of steak from Bill's plate while Bill's back was turned. How much food did Muffin consume?

    A. 1 pound 6 ounces
    B. 1 pound 4 ounces
    C. 1 pound 2 ounces
    D. 1 pound

26. Six friends agree to evenly split the cost of gasoline on a trip. Each friend paid $37.27. What was the total cost of gas?

    A. $370.27

B. $223.62
C. $314.78
D. $262.78

27. Fabio made quiche for dinner last night. He and his family ate 2/3 of it and saved the rest. The next day, Fabio ate 1/2 of the remainder for lunch. What fraction of the original quiche is left?

    A. 1/5
    B. 1/6
    C. 1/7
    D. 1/8

28. Pete earns only 1/8 what José does. José makes $19.50 an hour. For an 8-hour day, how much does Pete earn?

    A. $18.50
    B. $18.75
    C. $19.50
    D. $19.75

29. Carla has 20 math problems for homework. It takes her between 5 and 7 minutes to do each problem. Which is a reasonable estimate of the total number of minutes it will take her to do her math homework?

    A. 20 minutes
    B. 80 minutes
    C. 120 minutes
    D. 240 minutes

30. $(14 \times 7) + 12 =$

    A. 98
    B. 266
    C. 110
    D. 100

31. 2 feet 4 inches + 4 feet 8 inches=

    A. 6 feet 8 inches
    B. 7 feet
    C. 7 feet 12 inches
    D. 8 feet

32. 17^2=

    A. 34
    B. 68
    C. 136
    D. 289

33. 3.16 ÷ 0.079=

    A. 0.025
    B. 2.5
    C. 4.0
    D. 40.0

34. 300% of 20=

    A. 7
    B. 20
    C. 30
    D. 60

35. Solve for x in the following equation:
    x + 3= 8

    A. 33
    B. 15
    C. 11
    D. 3

36. Change this mixed number to an improper fraction: 5½

    A. 11/2
    B. 10/2
    C. 17/2
    D. 5/2

37. What is the perimeter of the polygon shown below?

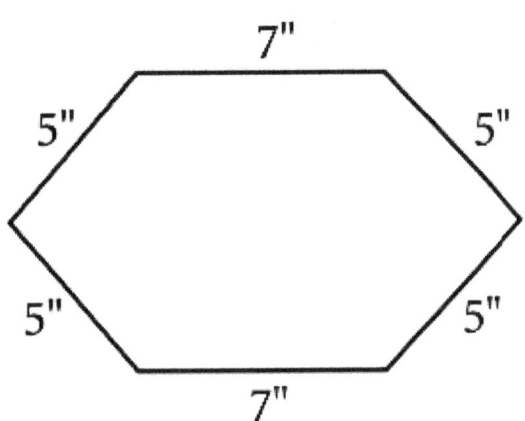

    A. 20 inches
    B. 27 inches
    C. 30 inches
    D. 34 inches

38. Mark's temperature at 9:00 A.M. was 97.2° F. At 4:00 P.M., his temperature was 99° F. By how many degrees did his temperature rise?

    A. 0.8° F
    B. 1.8° F
    C. 2.2° F
    D. 2.8° F

39. For the company's third anniversary, the caterer provided three 1-pound chunks of cheese. At the end of the party, there were 3/5 pound of Swiss, 4/7 pound of Vermont cheddar, and 5/8 pound of feta cheese left. What fraction of the original three pounds was left after the party?

   A. 1 123/280 pounds of cheese
   B. 1 223/280 pounds of cheese
   C. 1 283/270 pounds of cheese
   D. 1 393/290 pounds of cheese

40. Yetta just got a raise of 3¼%. Her original salary was $30,600. How much does she make now?

   A. $30,594.50
   B. $31,594.50
   C. $32,094.50
   D. $32,940.50

41. 7 ÷ 3/8=

   A. 18 ⅔
   B. 12 ⅜
   C. 14 ⅚
   D. 10 ⅘

42. s= t (3 + 5) − (11 − t)

   t= 2
   s=

   A. −7
   B. −5
   C. 5
   D. 7

43. 0.31 + 0.673=

   A. 0.0983

B. 0.983
C. 0.967
D. 9.83

44. The number of red blood corpuscles in one cubic millimeter is about 5,000,000, and the number of white blood corpuscles in one cubic millimeter is about 8,000. What, then, is the ratio of white blood corpuscles to red blood corpuscles?

    A. 1:625
    B. 1:40
    C. 4:10
    D. 5:1,250

45. In order to protect her new VW Bug, Maria needs to build a new garage. The concrete floor needs to be 64.125 square feet and is 9½ feet long. How wide does it need to be?

    A. 7.25 feet
    B. 5.5 feet
    C. 6.75 feet
    D. 8.25 feet

46. If $2x/16 = 12/48$, what is x?

    A. 2
    B. 3
    C. 4
    D. 5

47. The price of cheddar cheese is $2.12 per pound. The price of Monterey Jack cheese is $2.34 per pound. If Harrison buys 1.5 pounds of cheddar and 1 pound of Monterey Jack, how much will he spend in all?

    A. $3.18
    B. $4.46
    C. $5.41
    D. $5.52

48. After paying a commission to his broker of 7% of the sale price, a seller receives $103,000 for his house. How much did the house sell for?

   A. $95,790
   B. $110,000
   C. $110,420
   D. $110,753

49. This month, attendance at the baseball park was 150% of what it had been last month. If attendance this month was 280,000, what was the attendance last month, rounded to the nearest whole number?

   A. 140,000
   B. 176,670
   C. 186,667
   D. 205,556

50. Triangles RST and MNO are similar. What is the length of line segment MO?

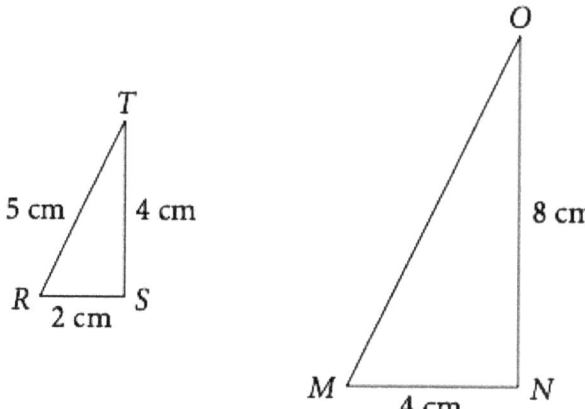

   A. 5 cm
   B. 10 cm
   C. 20 cm
   D. 32 cm

51. The sum of a number and its double is 69. What is the number?

    A. 46.6
    B. 34.5
    C. 23
    D. 20

52. If 10x − 3y = 40, and x = 1, what does y equal?

    A. −10
    B. −4
    C. 4
    D. 10

53. What is the median of the following group of numbers? 6, 8, 10, 12, 14, 16, 18

    A. 11
    B. 12
    C. 13
    D. 14

54. 35% of what number is equal to 14?

    A. 4
    B. 40
    C. 49
    D. 400

55. Which side is the longest of the following triangles, if triangle A is similar to triangle B?

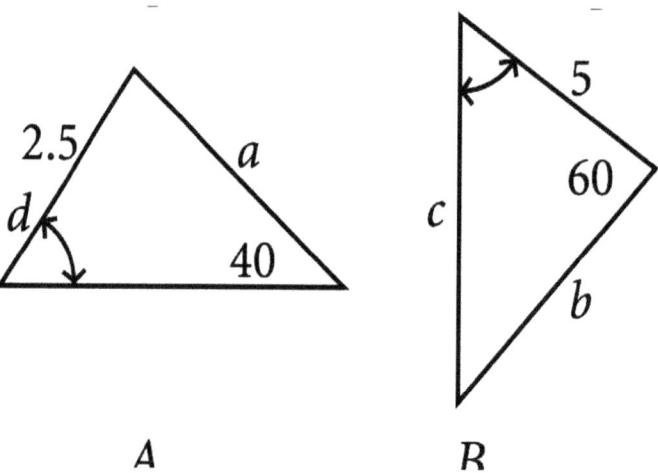

A. a
B. b
C. c
D. d

56. Of the 1,200 videos available for rent at a certain video store, 420 are comedies. What percent of the videos are comedies?

A. 28½%
B. 30%
C. 32%
D. 35%

57. One colony of bats consumes 36 tons of mosquitoes per year. At that rate, how many pounds of mosquitoes does the same colony consume in a month?

A. 36,000 pounds
B. 12,000 pounds
C. 6,000 pounds
D. 3,000 pounds

58. A helicopter flies over a river at 6:02 A.M. and arrives at a heliport 20 miles away at 6:17 A.M. How many miles per hour was the helicopter traveling?

   A. 120 mph
   B. 300 mph
   C. 30 mph
   D. 80 mph

59. Jared and Linda are both salespeople at a certain electronics store. If they made 36 sales one day, and Linda sold three less than twice Jared's sales total, how many units did Jared sell?

   A. 19
   B. 15
   C. 12
   D. 13

60. Karl is four times as old as Pam, who is one-third as old as Jackie. If Jackie is 18, what is the sum of their ages?

   A. 64
   B. 54
   C. 48
   D. 24

61. Solve for x in the following equation:
    $1.5x - 7 = 12.5$

   A. 29.25
   B. 19.5
   C. 13
   D. 5.5

62. What is the area of the rectangle?

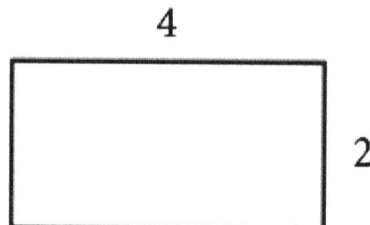

A. 6 square feet
B. 8 square feet
C. 12 square feet
D. 16 square feet

63. Gilda is making a quilt. She wants a quilt that is 30 square feet. She has collected fabric squares that are 6 inches by 6 inches. How many squares will she need?

A. 60 squares
B. 90 squares
C. 100 squares
D. 120 squares

64. 19 more than a certain number is 63. What is the number?

A. 14
B. 44
C. 58
D. 82

Part 5: Language Skills

Time: 25 minutes

Find the statement that has a capitalization, punctuation, or usage error for questions 1 through 40. Mark option d if there are no errors.

1.
   A. Where is Cuba on the map?
   B. Which continent, North America or South America, is larger?
   C. Hunter avenue runs along the Garden State Parkway.
   D. No mistakes.

2.
   A. The price of cereal has increased more than milk has.
   B. Samson and I left class at the same time.
   C. This winter is colder than last year's.
   D. d. No mistakes.

3.
   A. Henry's cousin came with us to the symphony.
   B. Whose at the door?
   C. "Don't forget your gloves," she said.
   D. No mistakes.

4.
   A. The first mistake was his last mistake.
   B. When the tiger pounced, it tenses its muscles.
   C. I need more sugar in my coffee.
   D. No mistakes.

5.
   A. My uncle drives a 1967 Eldorado Cadillac.
   B. The bride and groom dancing at their wedding.
   C. Put the packages on the counter.
   D. No mistakes.

6.

   A. "Sometimes," she said, you have to look closely."
   B. When we got to the bank, it was already closed.
   C. Allison is the best speller in school.
   D. No mistakes.

7.

   A. My favorite game when I was little was "Ring Around the Rosy."
   B. My mother's going to be so happy.
   C. Look before you leap.
   D. No mistakes.

8.

   A. "Shut the window. You're letting the heat out!" said Connor.
   B. A thesaurus will help you find another word that means the same.
   C. He didn't take no prisoners.
   D. No mistakes.

9.

   A. They weren't the only ones who didn't like the movie.
   B. "Please come back another time," Aunt Julie begged.
   C. "Threes a crowd," he always says.
   D. No mistakes.

10.

   A. Anne will head out first, and Nick will follow her.
   B. Maya Angelou, a famous poet, has recently directed a movie.
   C. The clerk asked for my address and phone number.
   D. No mistakes.

11.

   A. My cousin Randall is an artist and a musician.

B. I would love to live in Florida during the winter.
C. Margie wants to become a history professor.
D. No mistakes.

12.

A. Does Judge Parker live on your street?
B. Twenty government officials met to deal with Wednesday's crisis.
C. The Mayor spoke at a news conference this morning.
D. No mistakes.

13.

A. John Glenn was a senator from Ohio.
B. Is Dad going to join us for dinner?
C. Elizabeth I was one of England's most famous queens.
D. No mistakes.

14.

A. Indira sometimes wears her beautiful sari.
B. Lyle went shopping, and that he forgot his wallet.
C. His shoes are just like mine.
D. No mistakes.

15.

A. My brother Isaac is the best player on the team.
B. Because of the high cost; we decided not to go.
C. Where's your new puppy?
D. No mistakes.

16.

A. I have learned to appreciate Mozart's music.
B. My cousin Veronica is studying to be a Veterinarian.
C. Mr. Shanahan is taller than Professor Martin.
D. No mistakes.

17.
- A. We sold less cookies this year than we did last year.
- B. That parrot doesn't talk.
- C. Don't spend too much money.
- D. No mistakes.

18.
- A. She spread the frosting too thickly.
- B. "What is your answer?" she asked.
- C. We waited while he stopped to make a phone call.
- D. No mistakes.

19.
- A. Between the three of us, we should find the answer.
- B. Alberto laughed loudly when he saw us.
- C. They're looking for another apartment.
- D. No mistakes.

20.
- A. "You look just like your mother," Ms. Jones told me.
- B. "Please be careful," he said.
- C. Tyler asked, "why do I have to go to bed so early?"
- D. No mistakes.

21.
- A. The first house on the street is there's.
- B. I love the fireworks on the Fourth of July.
- C. My grandparents live in San Juan, Puerto Rico.
- D. No mistakes.

22.
- A. Graceland is the name of Elvis Presley's mansion.

B. We set up the tent, but it soon fell over.
C. Give me a break!
D. No mistakes.

23.

A. It has not rained since last April.
B. The jurors walked solemnly into the room.
C. Had we known, we would not have come.
D. No mistakes.

24.

A. The dog's barking woke us.
B. Ursula has broke one of your plates.
C. The sun rose from behind the mountain.
D. No mistakes.

25.

A. Do you prefer root beer over orange soda?
B. In which year did world war II end?
C. I like to study the geography of the Everglades.
D. No mistakes.

26.

A. After we sat down to eat dinner, the phone rung.
B. "Keep a positive attitude," he always says.
C. Sign here.
D. No mistakes.

27.

A. Colds like many other viruses are highly contagious.
B. Call me when you feel better.
C. Did you wash your hands, Michael?
D. No mistakes.

28.

    A. The Adirondacks are mountains in New York.
    B. President Carter gave the Panama Canal back to Panama.
    C. That river is terribly polluted.
    D. No mistakes.

29.

    A. The children's books are over there.
    B. She missed the bus and arrives late.
    C. There is hardly enough food for a mouse.
    D. No mistakes.

30.

    A. It's not my fault that you and him got caught.
    B. "Do you brush twice a day?" Dr. Evans asked.
    C. What's the weather report?
    D. No mistakes.

31.

    A. Couldn't you arrive fashionably late?
    B. You're assumption is correct.
    C. I know that Bowser will be well treated.
    D. No mistakes.

32.

    A. The industrial revolution began in Europe.
    B. Is Labor Day a national holiday?
    C. General Patton was a four-star general.
    D. No mistakes.

33.
- A. We invited Mayor Chen to speak at our school.
- B. The alarm sounded, and the firefighters jumped into the truck.
- C. The volunteers work as hard as one can.
- D. No mistakes.

34.
- A. The winners were announced yesterday.
- B. Liam is one of the boys who were chosen.
- C. Although Nick was not selected, he was happy for the others.
- D. No mistakes.

35.
- A. Carmen brought bread, and butter, and strawberry jam.
- B. Let's look at the map.
- C. Be sure to thank Aunt Helen for the gift.
- D. No mistakes.

36.
- A. He shook the crumbs from the tablecloth.
- B. We will strive to do our best.
- C. I see that Fred has wore his old shoes.
- D. No mistakes.

37.
- A. The Robber Bride is my favorite Margaret Atwood novel.
- B. I have never understood when to use dashes.
- C. What is this paragraph's topic sentence?
- D. No mistakes.

38.
- A. Opal likes to drive better than Claire does.

B. Clothes from the seventies are back in style.
C. Please write a note to Aunt Ginny.
D. No mistakes.

39.

A. My Aunt Georgia loves to read Eighteenth-Century novels.
B. Eli's sister's cousin lives in Alaska.
C. Is that a German shepherd?
D. No mistakes.

40.

A. Those shoes are too expensive.
B. Michael's best friend is Patrick.
C. Did you hear that Inez got a new puppy.
D. No mistakes.

Determine which phrase in questions 41–50 has a spelling error. Mark option D if there are no errors.

41.

A. All employees will be eligible for three weeks of vacation.
B. The managment team promised to look into the situation.
C. We saw an enormous animal running toward us.
D. No mistakes.

42.

A. The commissioner has assumed responsibility.
B. Kate likes to visit with her nieghbor.
C. This is not a commonly held viewpoint.
D. No mistakes.

43.

A. Edith and her sister closely resemble one another.

B. Her handwriting was barely legible.
C. There are two paring knifes in the drawer.
D. No mistakes.

44.

A. Our company sent forty representatives to the meeting.
B. When did you realize that the theory could not be proven?
C. We both filled out an application for employment.
D. No mistakes.

45.

A. All of the musicians were well trained.
B. Thank you for your assistance.
C. You are required to follow standard procee-dures.
D. No mistakes.

46.

A. I knew she was bored because she wriggled in her seat.
B. If you want to succeed, please report to work imediately.
C. He was conscious of his surroundings.
D. No mistakes.

47.

A. My mother will soon celebrate her fortieth birthday.
B. Autumn is my favorite time of year.
C. My cousin is going skiing in Feburary.
D. No mistakes.

48.

A. William is the most sensable person I know.
B. The festival is held at a different time each year.
C. It is not customary for the members to arrive late.
D. No mistakes.

49.
- A. As vice president of the student government, Judith is supposed to help the president.
- B. I recieved a passing grade in history.
- C. What a mess that toddler made!
- D. No mistakes.

50.
- A. Rachel remembered to ask the author a question.
- B. I vote in the election every November.
- C. Please pick up my perscription at the pharmacy.
- D. No mistakes.

Follow the instructions for each question for questions 51 through 60.

51. Choose the word that best joins the sentences.

    Everyone thought the game was lost. _____, at the last minute, the forward threw the ball into the basket and scored a victory.

    - A. Consequently
    - B. Thus
    - C. However
    - D. While

52. Choose the word that best joins the thoughts together.

    It's best if you take the highway _____ there are fewer potholes, which is better for your car.

    - A. because
    - B. nevertheless
    - C. and
    - D. but

53. Which of these expresses the idea most clearly?

    A. For three weeks, the Linden family was able to stick to their clothing and entertainment budgets.
    B. The Linden family, for three weeks, was able to stick to its clothing and entertainment budgets.
    C. The Linden family knew what their clothing and entertainment allowance was, but for three weeks, they did not know how to follow it.
    D. A clothing and entertainment allowance, for three weeks, was agreed upon by all members of the Linden family.

54. Which of these expresses the idea most clearly?

    A. There is no true relationship between ethics and the law.
    B. Ethics and the law having no true relationship.
    C. Between ethics and the law, no true relationship.
    D. Ethics and the law is no true relationship.

55. Which of these expresses the idea most clearly?

    A. Some students think walking to school is a waste of time and there should be a bus service.
    B. Bus service would save many students a long walk to school.
    C. A waste of time is walking to school is what many students would say.
    D. Having bus service, for many students, would be a good idea.

56. Choose the group of words that best completes this sentence.

    My neighbor, Mr. Christiansen, was such a skilled craftsman and woodworker that

    A. he received many awards at local craft shows and in magazines.
    B. he received many awards at local craft shows, and his work was featured in many magazines.
    C. he entered many local craft shows and awards, and then he had his work in many magazines.
    D. he entered his work in magazines and when he received awards at local craft shows.

57. Which of the following topics is best for a one-page essay?

   A. Computers in the Classroom
   B. Computer Projects Designed by Students
   C. How to Use Computers in the Classroom
   D. A Student-Designed Computer Project

58. Which of these best fits under the topic, "High Altitudes Increase Risks from the Sun"?

   A. Mountain athletes have always known that the thinner air at high altitudes means less oxygen.
   B. Researchers have found that ultraviolet radiation levels from the sun were 60 percent higher at 8,500 feet than they were at sea level.
   C. Fourteen minutes of noontime sun exposure in Orlando, Florida, is equal to twenty-five minutes in upstate New York.
   D. Dr. Darren, a dermatologist at the University Medical Center, is perfecting methods to heal skin that has been severely damaged by the sun.

59. Where should the sentence, "Because of these oxides and minerals, agates can be found in a multitude of colors," be placed in the paragraph below?

   1. The stones known as beach agates are a form of quartz.
   2. Thousands of years before the Ice Age, these agates formed in gravel beds along the coastal plains.
   3. They were formed by water-born silicones, oxides, and metals that were deposited in basalt and other earth forms.
   4. No two agates are exactly alike.

   A. before sentence 1
   B. between sentences 1 and 2
   C. between sentences 2 and 3
   D. between sentences 3 and 4

60. Which sentence does NOT belong in the paragraph?

   1. Barbara Miller stumbled upon her new business purely by accident.
   2. While she was visiting friends in Arizona, she happened to walk past

a dog bakery that sold all-natural dog biscuits, beaded collars, and canine gifts.
3. Veterinarians warn dog owners not to feed their pets people food.
4. Now, Miller is about to open her own dog bakery in New York.

A. sentence 1
B. sentence 2
C. sentence 3
D. sentence 4

Answer Key Verbal Skills

Q.	1	2	3	4	5	6	7	8	9	10
A.	B	A	A	D	B	D	A	C	D	C
Q.	11	12	13	14	15	16	17	18	19	20
A.	B	A	A	C	C	C	B	A	B	D
Q.	21	22	23	24	25	26	27	28	29	30
A.	D	A	A	C	C	D	A	B	A	B
Q.	31	32	33	34	35	36	37	38	39	40
A.	B	A	A	C	D	B	C	A	B	C
Q.	41	42	43	44	45	46	47	48	49	50
A.	C	D	D	A	B	B	C	D	C	D
Q.	51	52	53	54	55	56	57	58	59	60
A.	A	C	C	D	A	C	A	C	B	A

Answer Key Quantitative Skills

Q.	1	2	3	4	5	6	7	8	9	10
A.	C	D	A	B	A	B	A	A	B	C
Q.	11	12	13	14	15	16	17	18	19	20
A.	D	B	C	A	A	B	D	D	C	A
Q.	21	22	23	24	25	26	27	28	29	30
A.	C	D	B	B	D	D	C	D	A	B
Q.	31	32	33	34	35	36	37	38	39	40
A.	A	C	C	D	B	C	B	C	A	D
Q.	41	42	43	44	45	46	47	48	49	50
A.	C	A	A	B	D	D	B	C	B	B
Q.	51	52								
A.	B	C								

Answer Key Reading Skills

Q.	1	2	3	4	5	6	7	8	9	10
A.	B	C	B	C	C	A	B	B	C	B
Q.	11	12	13	14	15	16	17	18	19	20
A.	C	B	B	C	B	B	B	C	D	A
Q.	21	22	23	24	25	26	27	28	29	30
A.	B	C	C	B	B	B	C	B	A	B
Q.	31	32	33	34	35	36	37	38	39	40
A.	A	B	B	A	B	C	B	B	C	B

Answer Key Mathematics

Q.	1	2	3	4	5	6	7	8	9	10
A.	C	B	D	B	B	A	B	D	D	C
Q.	11	12	13	14	15	16	17	18	19	20
A.	D	A	C	C	A	B	A	D	A	C
Q.	21	22	23	24	25	26	27	28	29	30
A.	D	B	C	C	B	B	B	C	C	C
Q.	31	32	33	34	35	36	37	38	39	40
A.	B	D	D	D	B	A	D	B	B	B
Q.	41	42	43	44	45	46	47	48	49	50
A.	A	A	A	D	B	C	D	D	C	B
Q.	51	52	53	54	55	56	57	58	59	60
A.	C	A	B	B	B	D	C	D	D	C
Q.	61	62	63	64
A.	C	B	D	B

Answer Key Language Skills

Q.	1	2	3	4	5	6	7	8	9	10
A.	C	D	B	B	B	A	D	C	C	D
Q.	11	12	13	14	15	16	17	18	19	20
A.	D	C	D	B	B	B	A	D	A	C
Q.	21	22	23	24	25	26	27	28	29	30
A.	A	D	D	B	B	A	A	D	B	A
Q.	31	32	33	34	35	36	37	38	39	40
A.	B	A	C	B	A	C	D	B	A	C
Q.	41	42	43	44	45	46	47	48	49	50
A.	B	B	C	D	C	B	C	A	B	C
Q.	51	52	53	54	55	56	57	58	59	60
A.	C	A	A	A	B	B	D	B	C	D

Chapter Eight: Answers and Explanation of HSPT Exam 1

Part 1: Verbal Skills

1. **Answer**: B

    Explanation: A bed, dresser, and armoire are all pieces of furniture. Curtains, however, are not a piece of furniture.

2. **Answer**: A

    Explanation: Brick, steel, and wood are all materials commonly used for building structures. Paper is not a building material.

3. **Answer**: A

    Explanation: Since pistachios are the most expensive of the three types mentioned, the first two statements must be true.

4. **Answer**: D

    Explanation: A window consists of panes, while a book is made up of pages. A novel is a type of book, and glass has no relation to books. A cover is only one part of a book, not the whole.

5. **Answer**: B

    Explanation: A cup is a smaller unit of measurement than a gallon, just as a centimeter is a smaller unit than a meter. Yard, pint, and inch are either non-metric or do not fit the context.

6. **Answer**: D

    Explanation: Mutable and inconstant both suggest something that is subject to change, making them synonymous.

7. **Answer**: A

    Explanation: Perceptible and recognizable both refer to something that can be noticed or seen.

8. **Answer**: C

    Explanation: Unfortunate, sorrowful, and regrettable are all words that convey a sense of sadness or misfortune, making them synonyms.

9. **Answer**: D

    Explanation: Reality refers to something that exists in the real world, while imaginary refers to something that exists only in the mind.

10. **Answer**: C

    Explanation: A mouse is a type of rodent, just as an elm is a type of tree. A leaf and trunk are parts of a tree, not types of trees.

11. **Answer**: B

    Explanation: Elated is the opposite of despondent, and enlightened is the opposite of ignorant. Aware is a synonym of enlightened, making option b the best choice.

12. **Answer**: A

    Explanation: Curmudgeonly means someone who is difficult or irritable.

13. **Answer**: A

    Explanation: A rigorous schedule is one that is challenging, demanding, or difficult to follow.

14. **Answer**: C

    Explanation: The first two statements give information about the color of Joshua's socks. No conclusions can be drawn about other colors of socks.

15. **Answer**: C

    Explanation: Geology, zoology, and botany are scientific fields, while theology is the study of religion, not science.

16. **Answer**: C

    Explanation: Quadrilateral refers to a four-sided shape, while triangles have three sides.

17. **Answer**: B

    Explanation: Given the first two statements, Rebecca's house is to the northeast of the Shop-and-Save Grocery. Therefore, the third statement is false.

18. **Answer**: A

    Explanation: To be humiliated means to be greatly embarrassed, and terrified means to be extremely frightened. Agitated does not necessarily imply fear, and the other options don't reflect the emotional state of being terrified.

19. **Answer**: B

    Explanation: Exhaustive means thorough, while cursory means quick and not detailed.

20. **Answer**: D

    Explanation: An odometer is used to measure distance or mileage, and a compass is used to determine direction. The other options are unrelated tools.

21. **Answer**: D

    Explanation: A domain refers to a controlled area or territory, which is governed or administered, whereas territory refers to land under someone's responsibility.

22. **Answer**: A

    Explanation: To escalate means to increase in intensity, which is similar to the definition of intensify, making both words synonyms.

23. **Answer**: A

    Explanation: Based on the first two statements, Paws weighs the most and Tabby weighs the least, leading to the conclusion that the third statement is false.

24. **Answer**: C

    Explanation: While it's known that Harriet's succulents are flowering plants, it's not stated whether all succulents are flowering plants, so the statement cannot be verified.

25. **Answer**: C

    Explanation: Pecans, walnuts, and cashews are types of nuts, whereas a kernel is a part of a nut, not a type of nut.

26. **Answer**: D

    Explanation: Instruct, teach, and educate are all synonyms, as they all refer to the act of imparting knowledge.

27. **Answer**: A

    Explanation: Innocuous means something that is harmless or not offensive.

28. **Answer**: B

    Explanation: Intermittent refers to something that happens at irregular intervals, whereas constant refers to something that happens without interruption.

29. **Answer**: A

    Explanation: An optimist has a positive outlook, while a pessimist has a negative outlook. The other options don't fully capture the outlook of a pessimist.

30. **Answer**: B

    Explanation: The roof, door, and window are all parts of a house. The sidewalk is not part of the building.

31. **Answer**: B

    Explanation: Detrimental means something harmful or damaging.

32. **Answer**: A

    Explanation: Placid means calm or peaceful, and free of disturbance.

33. **Answer**: A

    Explanation: From the first two statements, it is clear that Signots with buttons are not Lamels, and yellow Signots cannot have buttons.

34. **Answer**: C

    Explanation: To demolish means to destroy or tear down, while to create means to build something up.

35. **Answer**: D

    Explanation: Notable means something that stands out or is unusual, while ordinary means something typical or usual.

36. **Answer**: B

    Explanation: The population of City A is the highest, so the third statement must be false.

37. **Answer**: C

    Explanation: Sardines, trout, and catfish are types of fish, while a lobster is a crustacean.

38. **Answer**: A

    Explanation: A synopsis is an abbreviated or condensed version of something, and a summary is a brief overview of facts or points.

39. **Answer**: B

    Explanation: Methodical means careful or systematic, while deliberate also means done carefully or slowly.

40. **Answer**: C

    Explanation: A scythe, knife, and saw are cutting tools, while pliers are used for gripping or bending, not cutting.

41. **Answer**: C

    Explanation: A sponge is porous, and rubber is elastic. The other options don't describe the main characteristics of rubber.

42. **Answer**: D

    Explanation: Candid means open and honest, while indirect and devious mean opposite of frank and truthful.

43. **Answer**: D

    Explanation: A recluse is someone who lives away from others, often in isolation, which aligns with the definition of a hermit.

44. **Answer**: A

    Explanation: The adjective novel refers to something new or different, not previously known.

45. **Answer**: B

    Explanation: Based on the first two statements, Bryant is sitting in front of Jerome and Martina, making the third statement false.

46. **Answer**: B

    Explanation: Two, six, and eight are even numbers, whereas three is an odd number.

47. **Answer**: C

    Explanation: Optimum refers to the best or most desirable condition, while worst refers to the least desirable condition.

48. **Answer**: D

    Explanation: Harmony refers to agreement, while conflict refers to disagreement.

49. **Answer**: C

    Explanation: A peninsula, island, and cape are landforms, while a bay is a body of water.

50. **Answer**: D

    Explanation: A pen is a tool for writing, just as a needle is a tool for sewing. The other options are not people and do not fit the analogy.

51. **Answer**: A

    Explanation: A rationale is the reasoning behind something, while an explanation is a clarification or definition of something.

52. **Answer**: C

    Explanation: To navigate and to steer both mean to guide or direct, often in the context of travel or movement.

53. **Answer**: C

    Explanation: The seat, rung, and leg are parts of a chair, but not all chairs are made of wood.

54. **Answer**: D

    Explanation: Fair, just, and equitable are all synonyms that refer to impartiality, whereas favorable refers to something showing approval or preference.

55. **Answer**: A

    Explanation: Bran cereal has more fiber than oat and corn cereals, and rice cereal has less fiber than both corn and wheat cereals. Therefore, rice cereal has the least fiber.

56. **Answer**: C

    Explanation: We know Jasmine weighs more than Jason, but we cannot determine if Jasmine weighs more than Jenna.

57. **Answer**: A

    Explanation: A malicious action and a spiteful action both aim to harm or hurt someone.

58. **Answer**: C

    Explanation: Defendant, prosecutor, and judge are all participants in a trial, while a trial itself is not a person.

59. **Answer**: B

    Explanation: Smile, laugh, and cry are all ways of actively showing or expressing emotions.

60. **Answer**: A

    Explanation: To disperse means to scatter, whereas to gather means to bring together or collect.

Part 2: Quantitative Skills

1. **Answer:** C

   Explanation: This is an alternating-with-repetition series, in which each number repeats itself, then increases by 6.

2. **Answer:** D

   Explanation: The rectangles are all the same size and all are one-half shaded.

3. **Answer:** A

   Explanation: First, solve for (A), (B), and (C): 3 × (3 + 1) = 12; 1 × (4 + 6) = 10; 2 × (9 + 3) = 24. Then find out which choice is true.

4. **Answer:** B

   Explanation: 1/2 of 22 = 11; 6 + 11 = 17.

5. **Answer:** A

   Explanation: 10% of 60= 6; 6 divided by 2= 3.

6. **Answer:** B

   Explanation: Count the number of diamonds in (A), (B), and (C) and then test each choice to find out if it is true.

7. **Answer:** A

   Explanation: This is an alternating addition and subtraction series. In the first pattern, 10 is subtracted from each number to arrive at the next. In the second, 5 is added to each number to arrive at the next.

8. **Answer:** A

   Explanation: First, change (B) and (C) to decimals: 5%= 0.05; 1/5= 0.2. Then find out which choice is true.

9. **Answer:** B

   Explanation: This is a simple subtraction series; each number is 7 less than the previous number.

10. **Answer:** C

    Explanation: First, set up the equation: n ÷ 4= 1/2 of 6. Then solve: n ÷ 4= 3; n= 12.

11. **Answer:** D

    Explanation: 25% of 8= 2; 2 + 10= 12.

12. **Answer:** B

    Explanation: In this addition series, 10 is added to the first number, 11 is added to the second number, 12 is added to the third number, and so forth.

13. **Answer:** C

    Explanation: This is a simple addition series. Each number increases by 1/6.

14. **Answer:** A

    Explanation: The figure forms two right triangles. Line AD is the hypotenuse and must be longer than either AB or CD.

15. **Answer:** A

    Explanation: 1/9 of 45= 5; 5 − 6= −1.

16. **Answer:** B

    Explanation: First, solve for (A), (B), and (C): (A)= 40, (B)= 40, (C)= 20. Then find out which choice is true.

17. **Answer:** D

    Explanation: This is a simple addition series; each number is 3 more than the previous number.

18. **Answer:** D

    Explanation: First, determine the value of each letter: A= 12, B= 3, C= 9, D= 15. Then test each choice to find out if it is true.

19. **Answer:** C

    Explanation: 2/5 of 25= 10; 10 − 6= 4.

20. **Answer:** A

    Explanation: 4% of 20= 0.8; 3 × 0.8= 2.4.

21. **Answer:** C

    Explanation: This is a multiplication series; each number is 3 times the previous number.

22. **Answer:** D

    Explanation: (B) and (C) are equal to n × n.

23. **Answer:** B

    Explanation: First, set up the equation: 9 + n= 6 × 5. Then, solve: n= 30 − 9; n= 21.

24. **Answer:** B

    Explanation: This is an alternating subtraction series. First, 2 is subtracted, then 4, then 2, and so on.

25. **Answer:** D

    Explanation: First, determine the amounts shown in (A), (B), and (C), and then test each statement to find out if it is true.

26. **Answer:** D

    Explanation: Of (A), (B), and (C), each is equal to 3.

27. **Answer:** C

    Explanation: In this alternating repetition series, the random number 21 is interpolated every other number into an otherwise simple addition series that increases by 2, beginning with the number 9.

28. **Answer:** D

    Explanation: In this simple subtraction series, each number decreases by 0.4.

29. **Answer:** A

    Explanation: First, set up the equation: n ÷ 5= 1/10 × 300. Then solve: n ÷ 5= 30; n= 150.

30. **Answer:** B

    Explanation: There are two series here, with every third term following the second pattern. The main series begins with 2, and 3 is added to each number to arrive at the next. The second series begins with 28, and 8 is subtracted from each number to arrive at the next.

31. **Answer:** A

    Explanation: AC plus BD are equal to 2x and are therefore less than AB, which is 3x.

32. **Answer:** C

    Explanation: First, solve for (A), (B), and (C): (A)= 49, (B)= 64, (C)= 15. Then find out which choice is true.

33. **Answer:** C

    Explanation: This is a simple alternating addition and subtraction series. In the first pattern, 3 is added; in the second, 2 is subtracted.

34. **Answer:** D

    Explanation: First, set up the equation: (0.15 × 30) + n= 20. Then solve: 4.5 + n= 20; n= 15.5.

35. **Answer:** B

    Explanation: Count the number of blocks in (A), (B), and (C), and then test each choice to find out which one is true.

36. **Answer:** C

    Explanation: This is a simple multiplication series. Each number is three times more than the previous number.

37. **Answer:** B

    Explanation: First, set up the equation: n + 2n= 99. Then solve: 3n= 99; n= 33.

38. **Answer:** C

    Explanation: 12% of 1,000= 120; 120 + 16= 136.

39. **Answer**: A

    Explanation: This is a simple division series. Each number is divided by 5.

40. **Answer**: D

    Explanation: First, solve for (B) and (C): (B)= 30, (C)= 12. Then find out which choice is true.

41. **Answer**: C

    Explanation: Angle (A) is a right triangle. Angle (B) plus angle (C) equals another right triangle.

42. **Answer**: A

    Explanation: In this series, the letters progress by 1; the numbers increase by 3.

43. **Answer**: A

    Explanation: This is an alternating multiplication and addition series: First, divide by 2, and then add 8.

44. **Answer**: B

    Explanation: First, set up the equation: $7n = (0.6 \times 770) \div 6$. Then solve: $7n = 77$; $n = 11$.

45. **Answer**: D

    Explanation: First, set up the equation: $33 = 0.12 \times n$. Then solve: $33 \div 0.12 = 275$.

46. **Answer**: D

    Explanation: This is an alternating multiplication series. Each number is

2 times more than the previous number. Roman numbers alternate with Arabic numbers.

47. **Answer:** B

    Explanation: First, determine an approximate percentage for each letter: A= 25%, B= 5%, C= 15%, D= 22%, E= 33%. Then, test each statement to find out if it is true.

48. **Answer:** C

    Explanation: 1/5 of 820= 164; 164 − 42= 122.

49. **Answer:** B

    Explanation: In this simple addition with repetition series, each number in the series repeats itself, and then increases by 11 to arrive at the next number.

50. **Answer:** B

    Explanation: First, convert (B) and (C) to inches: (B)= 15 inches and (C)= 37 inches. Then, find out which choice is true.

51. **Answer:** B

    Explanation: This is a simple subtraction series in which the random number 85 is interpolated as every third number. In the subtraction series, 10 is subtracted from each number to arrive at the next.

52. **Answer:** C

    Explanation: First, set up the equation: $n \div 4 = 8 + (4 \times 2)$. Then, solve: $n \div 4 = 16$; $n = 64$.

Part 3: Reading Skills

Passage 1:

1. **Answer**: B

   Explanation: The passage highlights that bats help control insect populations by eating hundreds of mosquitoes, which benefits humans and ecosystems.

2. **Answer**: C

   Explanation: Echolocation is described as a biological sonar that allows bats to navigate and hunt by emitting sound waves and interpreting the returning echoes.

3. **Answer**: B

   Explanation: The passage states that fruit bats play a crucial role in pollination and seed dispersal, benefiting plants like bananas and mangoes.

4. **Answer**: C

   Explanation: The passage mentions white-nose syndrome as a significant disease affecting bat populations, along with habitat loss and climate change.

5. **Answer**: C

   Explanation: Bats are beneficial because they eat mosquitoes, which can carry diseases, as stated in the passage.

6. **Answer**: A

   Explanation: The main purpose of the passage is to educate readers about the role bats play in ecosystems and the need for their conservation.

Passage 2:

7. **Answer:** B

   Explanation: The passage compares coral reefs to rainforests because of their incredible biodiversity, supporting 25% of all marine species.

8. **Answer:** B

   Explanation: The symbiotic relationship between zooxanthellae and coral involves the algae performing photosynthesis to supply energy to the coral.

9. **Answer:** C

   Explanation: The passage states that coral reefs protect coastal areas from storm surges and erosion, support fishing industries, and attract tourists.

10. **Answer:** B

    Explanation: Coral bleaching occurs when corals expel the algae living in their tissues due to stress, turning white and often leading to their death.

11. **Answer:** C

    Explanation: Marine protected areas are mentioned as a conservation effort, not a threat to coral reefs.

12. **Answer:** B

    Explanation: The main purpose of the passage is to educate readers about the ecological significance of coral reefs and the challenges they face.

Passage 3:

13. **Answer:** B

    Explanation: The passage defines AI as the ability of machines to perform tasks that typically require human intelligence, such as problem-solving and decision-making.

14. **Answer**: C

    Explanation: The passage explains that AI systems use machine learning, which involves analyzing vast amounts of data to identify patterns and improve performance.

15. **Answer**: B

    Explanation: While the passage highlights uses like fraud detection, medical imaging, and recommendation systems, it does not mention creating music.

16. **Answer**: B

    Explanation: Ethical concerns, such as bias and job displacement, are noted as reasons why AI's rise is controversial.

17. **Answer**: B

    Explanation: The passage mentions that AI can combat climate change by optimizing energy use and improving healthcare access.

18. **Answer**: C

    Explanation: The passage emphasizes balancing innovation with ethical responsibility to maximize the benefits of AI while addressing its challenges.

Passage 4

19. **Answer**: D

    Explanation: The passage states that over 80% of the world's oceans remain unexplored, highlighting the vastness of the unknown in deep-sea environments.

20. **Answer:** A

    Explanation: The "midnight zone" is described as the region below 200 meters where sunlight cannot penetrate, resulting in darkness.

21. **Answer:** B

    Explanation: The passage mentions ROVs, along with AUVs and submersibles, as key technologies enabling deep ocean exploration.

22. **Answer:** C

    Explanation: Oceans play a critical role in climate regulation by absorbing carbon dioxide and redistributing heat across the planet, as described in the passage.

23. **Answer:** C

    Explanation: The passage highlights human activities such as deep-sea mining and plastic pollution as major threats to fragile deep-sea ecosystems.

24. **Answer:** B

    Explanation: The central theme of the passage emphasizes the importance of exploring and protecting the deep ocean to unlock its benefits and preserve its ecosystems.

Passage 5:

25. **Answer:** B

    Explanation: The fire triangle consists of heat, fuel, and oxygen, which are necessary for a fire to ignite and sustain itself.

26. **Answer:** B

    Explanation: The passage advises testing smoke alarms monthly to ensure they are functioning properly.

27. **Answer:** C

    Explanation: The most important rule in case of a fire is to prioritize safety by leaving the building and contacting emergency services.

28. **Answer:** B

    Explanation: Cooking is highlighted as one of the leading causes of house fires, emphasizing the need to stay attentive while preparing food.

29. **Answer:** A

    Explanation: Knowing fire exits is crucial for safely evacuating a building in case of an emergency.

30. **Answer:** B

    Explanation: The central message emphasizes the importance of taking preventive steps and staying informed to reduce fire risks.

31. **Answer:** A

    Explanation: The passage highlights that electrical fires often result from overloaded outlets, frayed wires, or malfunctioning appliances. Regular inspections and avoiding the use of damaged equipment are key to reducing this risk.

32. **Answer:** B

    Explanation: The passage emphasizes that the most important rule during a fire is to "get out and stay out." Attempting to retrieve belongings can lead to dangerous situations, risking lives unnecessarily.

Passage 6

33. **Answer**: B

    Explanation: The passage explains that acupuncture aims to stimulate the flow of "qi" to promote balance and well-being.

34. **Answer**: A

    Explanation: Meridians are described as pathways through which energy travels in traditional Chinese medicine.

35. **Answer**: B

    Explanation: Acupuncture is commonly used for chronic pain, stress, anxiety, and related conditions.

36. **Answer**: C

    Explanation: Modern science suggests that acupuncture affects the nervous system and triggers the release of pain-relieving chemicals.

37. **Answer**: B

    Explanation: Using sterile needles minimizes the risk of infection and ensures patient safety, as noted in the passage.

38. **Answer**: B

    Explanation: The main idea highlights acupuncture's role in integrating traditional and modern healthcare practices.

39. **Answer**: C

    Explanation: The passage mentions that many patients report feelings of calmness and improved well-being after acupuncture sessions, highlighting its benefits beyond physical pain relief.

40. **Answer**: B

    Explanation: The passage emphasizes that acupuncture is not a "cure-all" but is valuable as a complementary treatment, bridging traditional practices with modern healthcare.

Part 4: Mathematics

1. **Answer**: C

   Explanation: The correct answer here is 10,447. It helps, if you are in a place where you can do so, to read the answer aloud; that way, you'll likely catch any mistake. When writing numbers with more than 4 digits, begin at the right and separate the digits into groups of threes with commas.

2. **Answer**: B

   Explanation: The variable is a symbol that stands for any number under discussion.

3. **Answer**: D

   Explanation: The hundredths place is two digits to the right of the decimal point. The 9 is in the tenths place; the 0 is in the thousandths place; the 2 is in the ten-thousandths place.

4. **Answer**: B

   Explanation: Fractions must be converted to the lowest common denominator, which is 60. $6/10 = 36/60$; $11/20 = 8/15$; $8/15 = 32/60$, which is the smallest fraction.

5. **Answer**: B

   Explanation: $62.5\% = 62.5/100$. You should multiply both the numerator and denominator by 10 to move the decimal point, resulting in $625/1000 = (5*5*5*5)/$

(5 *5*5**8) and then factor both the numerator and denominator to find out how far you can reduce the fraction. After cancelling the three 5s, you get 5/8.

6. **Answer:** A

   Explanation: A straight angle is exactly 180 degrees.

7. **Answer:** B

   Explanation: We multiply –6 by itself and get (–6) × (–6). When multiplying two negative numbers, the answer is always positive: 36.

8. **Answer:** D

   Explanation: To find the answer, do the following equation: 11 × 0.032 = 0.352.

9. **Answer:** D

   Explanation: This is the only choice that includes a 90-degree angle.

10. **Answer:** C

    Explanation: There are 16 ounces in one pound, so the ratio of 2 ounces to 1 pound is 2:16. Reduced, this becomes 1:8.

11. **Answer:** D

    Explanation: First, change the names to letters; remember that the letters then represent, not the people, but their ages. S (Salwa's age) equals R (Roland's age) plus 10 (years).

12. **Answer:** A

    Explanation: Change the mixed number to an improper fraction: 3¾ = 15/4. Now invert: 4/15.

13. **Answer:** C

    Explanation: The solution to this problem lies in knowing that 1002 is equal to 100 × 100, or 10,000. Next, you must multiply 10,000 × 2.75 to arrive at 27,500.

14. **Answer:** C

    Explanation: Complementary angles add to 90 degrees. Therefore, the complementary angle is 90 – 36 = 54 degrees.

15. **Answer:** A

    Explanation: The symbol > means "greater than," and the symbol < means "less than." The only sentence that is correct is choice a: 4 feet is greater than 3 feet. The other choices are untrue.

16. **Answer:** B

    Explanation: The other choices are all untrue.

17. **Answer:** A

    Explanation: This is the only common factor.

18. **Answer:** D

    Explanation: A quadrilateral is a polygon with four sides. This eliminates the triangle. Rectangles, squares, and parallelograms all have two parallel sides, but only a parallelogram can have an angle that measures something other than 90 degrees.

19. **Answer:** A

    Explanation: 10^{18} means 10 to the 18th power, or 10 times itself 18 times.

20. **Answer:** C

    Explanation: The greatest area from a quadrilateral will always be a square. Therefore, a side will be 24 ÷ 4= 6 feet. The area is 6^2= 36 square feet.

21. **Answer:** D

    Explanation: The hundredths place is two decimals over from the decimal point. If the digit to the right of it is less than 5, do not round up.

22. **Answer:** B

    Explanation: Since 0.05 = 1/20, 0.05 is greater than 1/25.

23. **Answer:** C

    Explanation: There are 4 quarts to a gallon; 2 pints to a quart; 2 cups to a pint.

24. **Answer:** C

    Explanation: The perimeter is 4 × 4 for the square, and the circumference is dπ for the circle. This is a difference of 16 - 4π.

25. **Answer:** B

    Explanation: This is a basic addition problem. Begin by adding: 14 ounces + 6 ounces = 20 ounces. Since there are 16 ounces in a pound, 20 ounces becomes 1 pound 4 ounces.

26. **Answer:** B

    Explanation: $37.27 × 6= $223.62.

27. **Answer:** B

    Explanation: There is ⅓ of the quiche left after the first day. ½ of ⅓ = ½ × ⅓ = ⅙

28. **Answer:** C

   Explanation: First, change the fraction to a decimal: 1/8 = 1 ÷ 8= 0.125. Now multiply that by José's hourly wage in order to get Pete's hourly wage: 0.125 × $19.50= $2.4375 (rounded). Now multiply Pete's hourly wage by 8 hours. $2.4375 × 8= $19.50.

29. **Answer:** C

   Explanation: On average, it takes Carla about 6 minutes to do each math problem. Multiplying 6 minutes by 20 problems gives an answer of about 120 minutes to do her math homework.

30. **Answer:** C

   Explanation: Perform the operation in parentheses first: 14 × 7= 98, and then add 12 to get the answer, which is 110.

31. **Answer:** B

   Explanation: Add the feet first, then the inches: 2 feet + 4 feet= 6 feet. Then, 4 inches + 8 inches= 12 inches. Convert 12 inches into 1 foot to get the correct answer 6 feet + 1 foot= 7 feet.

32. **Answer:** D

   Explanation: 17^2 means 17 squared and is equivalent to 17 × 17, which equals 289.

33. **Answer:** D

   Explanation: This is a simple division problem with decimals.

34. **Answer:** D

   Explanation: Convert the percent to a decimal, so that it becomes 3.0. Now multiply: 20 × 3.0= 60.

35. **Answer:** B

    Explanation: x + 3= 8. In order to solve the equation, all numbers need to be on one side and all x values on the other. Therefore, x = 5; x= 15.

36. **Answer:** A

    Explanation: Multiply the whole number by the fraction's denominator. 5 × 2 = 10. Add the fraction's numerator to the answer: 1 + 10 = 11. Now place that answer over the fraction's denominator: 11/2.

37. **Answer:** D

    Explanation: The sum of the measurements is the perimeter. This is 4 × 5 inches + 2 × 7 inches.

38. **Answer:** B

    Explanation: This is a simple subtraction problem. Be sure to align the decimal points. 99.0 − 97.2= 1.8.

39. **Answer:** B

    Explanation: The common denominator of the fractions is 280. The sum of the fractions is $503/280$, or $1\,223/280$.

40. **Answer:** B

    Explanation: First, change the percent to a decimal: 3¼% = 3.25% = 0.0325. Now multiply: 30,600 × 0.0325 = 994.5. Finally, add: $30,600 + 994.50 = $31,594.50 for Yetta's current salary.

41. **Answer:** A

    Explanation: The unreduced ratio is 8,000:5,000,000; reduced, the ratio is 8:5,000. Now divide: 5,000 ÷ 8 = 625, for a ratio of 1:625.

42. **Answer:** A

    Explanation: Cross multiplying: (2x)(48) = (16)(12); 96x= 192. Thus, x= 2.

43. **Answer:** A

    Explanation: The correct answer is 182/3.

44. **Answer:** D

    Explanation: s= (2 × 8) − (11 − 2); s= 16 − (11 − 2); s= 16 − 9; s= 7

45. **Answer:** B

    Explanation: The last digit has to be a 3, which rules out c. You can rule out a and d because of their place values.

46. **Answer:** C

    Explanation: The formula for area is area= length × width, in this case, 64.125= 9.5 × width, or 6.75.

47. **Answer:** D

    Explanation: This problem requires both multiplication and addition. First, multiply 2.12 by 1.5 to find the price of the cheddar cheese: 2.12 × 1.5= 3.18. Then add: 2.12 + 2.34= 5.52.

48. **Answer:** D

    Explanation: The seller's $103,000 represents only 93% of the sale price (100% − 7%). The broker's commission is NOT 7% of $103,000, but rather 7% of the whole sale price. The question is: $103,000 is 93% of what figure? So, let x= 103,000 ÷ 93= 110,752.68, rounded to $110,753.

49. **Answer:** C

    Explanation: This percent problem involves finding the whole when the percent is given. 280,000 is 150% of last month's attendance. Convert 150% to a decimal: 150%= 1.5. 280,000= 1.5 × LMA. Next, divide: 280,000 ÷ 1.5= 186,666.6666. Round up to the nearest whole number: 186,667.

50. **Answer:** B

    Explanation: The dimensions of triangle MNO are double those of triangle RST. Line segment RT is 5 cm; therefore, line segment MO is 10 cm.

51. **Answer:** C

    Explanation: If the number is represented by n, its double is 2n. Therefore, n + 2n= 69; 3n= 69; n= 23.

52. **Answer:** A

    Explanation: 10 - 3y= 40; - 3y = 30; y= - 10.

53. **Answer:** B

    Explanation: The median is merely the number in the middle of the series when the numbers are arranged in order, which, in this case, is 12.

54. **Answer:** B

    Explanation: Change the percent to a decimal: 0.35; then, to find the answer, divide: 14 ÷ 0.35= 40.

55. **Answer:** B

    Explanation: Since the 5-inch side and the 2.5-inch side are similar, the second triangle must be larger than the first. The two angles without congruent marks add up to 100 degrees, so 180 - 100= 80 degrees. This is the largest angle, so the side opposite it must be largest, in this case, side b.

56. **Answer:** D

   Explanation: To find what percent one number is of another, first write out an equation. Since x%= x/100, the equation is: =420/1200. Cross-multiply to find 1200x= (420) (100). Simplify : x= . Thus x= 35, meaning 35% of the videos are comedies.

57. **Answer:** C

   Explanation: First, convert tons to pounds. 1 ton= 2,000 pounds. 36 tons (per year)= 72,000 pounds (per year). 1 year= 12 months, so the average number of pounds of mosquitoes the colony of bats can consume in a month is: 72,000 ÷ 12= 6,000 pounds.

58. **Answer:** D

   Explanation: We want to know R= helicopter's speed in mph. Recall that rate × time= distance. T= 6:17 – 6:02 = 15 minutes = 0.25 hour, and D= 20 miles. Substituting, R × 0.25= 20. Simplifying: R= 20 ÷ 0.25, so R= 80 mph.

59. **Answer:** D

   Explanation: The total sales equal the sum of Linda and Jared's sales: L + J= 36. Since Linda sold three less than twice Jared's total, L= 2J – 3. The equation (2J – 3) + J= 36 models this situation. This gives 3J= 39; J= 13.

60. **Answer:** C

   Explanation: Karl is four times as old as Pam means K= 4P, and Pam is one-third as old as Jackie means P= ⅓ of J. We are given J= 18. Working backward, P= ⅓(18) = 6; K= 4(6)= 24. The sum of their ages= K + P + J = 24 + 6 + 18 = 48.

61. **Answer:** C

   Explanation: Seven is added to both sides of the equation, giving 1.5x= 19.5. 19.5 ÷ 1.5= 13.

62. **Answer:** B

    Explanation: Area is equal to base times height. 2 × 4= 8.

63. **Answer:** D

    Explanation: Each quilt square is 1/4 of a square foot. 6 inches is 1/2 a foot, so 0.5 × 0.5 = 0.25 square feet. Therefore, each square foot of the quilt requires 4 quilt squares. 30 square feet × 4= 120 quilt squares.

64. **Answer:** B

    Explanation: Let x= the number sought. Nineteen more than a certain number is 63 means: x + 19 = 63, or x= 63 − 19. Thus, x= 44.

Part 5: Language Skills

1. **Answer:** C

    Explanation: Avenue should be capitalized.

2. **Answer:** D

    Explanation: All the answers are correct.

3. **Answer:** B

    Explanation: Whose is possessive. The contraction Who's is correct.

4. **Answer:** B

    Explanation: This sentence contains a shift in tense, from past to present.

5. **Answer:** B

   Explanation: The verb does not agree with the subject. The subject is plural and requires the word are.

6. **Answer:** A

   Explanation: To set off the dialogue, there should be quotation marks before the word "you."

7. **Answer:** D

   Explanation: All the answers are correct.

8. **Answer:** C

   Explanation: This sentence contains a double negative.

9. **Answer:** C

   Explanation: The contraction "Three's," which means "Three is," is the correct usage.

10. **Answer:** D

    Explanation: All the answer choices are correct.

11. **Answer:** D

    Explanation: All the answer choices are correct.

12. **Answer:** C

    Explanation: Mayor should not be capitalized because it does not refer to a particular mayor.

13. **Answer:** D

    Explanation: All the answer choices are correct.

14. **Answer:** B

    Explanation: This sentence has a faulty shift in construction; the word "that" should be omitted from the sentence.

15. **Answer:** B

    Explanation: A semicolon is not used between a dependent and an independent clause. Use a comma or no punctuation.

16. **Answer:** B

    Explanation: Veterinarian is not a proper noun and should not be capitalized.

17. **Answer:** A

    Explanation: This sentence has a usage error: fewer cookies, not less cookies.

18. **Answer:** D

    Explanation: All the answer choices are correct.

19. **Answer:** A

    Explanation: Between is only used to refer to two things. Among them is the correct word to use in this sentence.

20. **Answer:** C

    Explanation: The word "Why," which begins the quotation, should be capitalized.

21. **Answer:** A

    Explanation: The correct usage is the possessive "theirs," not "there's."

22. **Answer:** D

    Explanation: All the answer choices are correct.

23. **Answer:** D

    Explanation: All the answer choices are correct.

24. **Answer:** B

    Explanation: The correct verb form is "has broken."

25. **Answer:** B

    Explanation: "World War" is a proper noun and should be capitalized.

26. **Answer:** A

    Explanation: The correct verb form is "rang."

27. **Answer:** A

    Explanation: The phrase "like many other viruses" should be set off by commas because it is a nonessential element in the sentence.

28. **Answer:** D

    Explanation: All the answer choices are correct.

29. **Answer:** B

    Explanation: There is an illogical shift in tense. Both verbs should be in the past tense.

30. **Answer:** A

    Explanation: The pronoun "him" is incorrect. "He" should be used because "you" and "he" are the subjects of the dependent clause.

31. **Answer:** B

    Explanation: The contraction "You're" should be replaced with the possessive "Your."

32. **Answer:** A

    Explanation: "Industrial Revolution" should be capitalized.

33. **Answer:** C

    Explanation: This sentence makes a shift in person. It should read: "The volunteers work as hard as they can."

34. **Answer:** B

    Explanation: The verb should agree with "one," not "boys"; so the singular verb "was" should be used.

35. **Answer:** A

    Explanation: The commas in this sentence should be deleted. Commas are not used in a series when the series is already linked by conjunctions.

36. **Answer:** C

    Explanation: The correct verb form is "has worn."

37. **Answer:** D

    Explanation: All the answer choices are correct.

38. **Answer:** D

    Explanation: All the answer choices are correct.

39. **Answer:** A

    Explanation: The names of centuries are not capitalized.

40. **Answer:** C

    Explanation: This sentence asks a question and should end with a question mark.

41. **Answer:** B

    Explanation: "Management" is the correct spelling.

42. **Answer:** B

    Explanation: "Neighbor" is the correct spelling.

43. **Answer:** C

    Explanation: "Knives" is the correct spelling.

44. **Answer:** D

    Explanation: All the words are spelled correctly.

45. **Answer:** C

    Explanation: "Procedures" is the correct spelling.

46. **Answer:** B

    Explanation: "Immediately" is the correct spelling.

47. **Answer:** C

   Explanation: "February" is the correct spelling.

48. **Answer:** A

   Explanation: "Sensible" is the correct spelling.

49. **Answer:** B

   Explanation: "Received" is the correct spelling.

50. **Answer:** C

   Explanation: "Prescription" is the correct spelling.

51. **Answer:** C

   Explanation: This is the only choice that is logical. The other choices imply a cause and effect that does not exist.

52. **Answer:** A

   Explanation: This is the only choice that shows a cause and effect between the two parts of the sentence.

53. **Answer:** A

   Explanation: The other choices are awkwardly constructed and difficult to read.

54. **Answer:** A

   Explanation: Answers b and c are sentence fragments. Answer d represents confused sentence structure as well as lack of agreement between subject and verb.

55. **Answer:** B

   Explanation: This choice most clearly states the advantage of having bus service.

56. **Answer:** B

   Explanation: This is the only choice that states the information clearly.

57. **Answer:** D

   Explanation: The other choices are much too broad to be adequately covered in a short essay.

58. **Answer:** B

   Explanation: This is the best choice because it is the only one that refers to risks from the sun at high altitudes. Choice a has nothing to do with risks from the sun; c gives no reference to high altitudes; d is about healing, not sun risk.

59. **Answer:** C

   Explanation: This sentence shifts the topic away from Barbara Miller and her dog bakery.

60. **Answer:** D

   Explanation: This is the only logical choice. This new sentence could not logically appear before sentence 3 because sentence 3 introduces the oxides and minerals.

Conclusion

Congratulations on completing your preparation with the *HSPT Prep Book 2025-2026 for Catholic Schools*! By now, you should have a solid understanding of the key concepts covered on the exam and have practiced with the same types of questions you'll face.

Remember, consistent review and self-assessment are key to ensuring your success. We wish you the best of luck as you take the next step toward your academic future. Stay confident, stay focused, and know that your hard work will pay off!

References

2022. In *HSPT Prep Book 2022-2023 - Secrets Study Guide for the Catholic High School Placement Test, Full-Length Practice Exam, Step-By-Step Video Tutorials: [3rd Edition]*, edited by Matthew Bowling. N.p.: Mometrix Media LLC.

Cox, Jonathan. 2023. *HSPT Prep Book 2024-2025: 700+ Practice Questions and Study Guide for the Catholic High School Placement Test*. N.p.: Accepted, Incorporated.

Elevate Prep. 2020. In *HSPT: 2500+ Practice Questions*. N.p.: Independently Published.

M, Justin. 2023. In *The Essential Guide to HSPT/ TACHS/ COOP Reading*.

Mometrix School Admissions Test Team, ed. 2010. *HSPT Secrets Study Guide: HSPT Exam Review for the High School Placement Test*. N.p.: Mometrix Media LLC.

Mometrix School Admissions Test Team, ed. 2015. *HSPT Practice Questions: HSPT Practice Tests & Exam Review for the High School Placement Test*. N.p.: Mometrix Media LLC.

Nazari, Reza, and Ava Ross. 2019. *5 Full-Length HSPT Math Practice Tests: The Practice You Need to Ace the HSPT Math Test*. N.p.: Effortless Math Education.